I0108181

Calvinism in History

CALVINISM IN HISTORY
A Political, Moral and Evangelizing Force

by

Nathaniel S. McFetridge

Solid Ground Christian Books
Birmingham, Alabama USA

SOLID GROUND CHRISTIAN BOOKS
PO Box 660132, Vestavia Hills, AL 35266
205-443-0311
sgcb@charter.net
http://www.solid-ground-books.com

Calvinism in History
A Political, Moral & Evangelizing Force

by Nathaniel Smyth McFetridge

First published in 1882 by Presbyterian Board of Publication

Published by Solid Ground Christian Books

Classic Reprints Series

First printing November 2004

ISBN: 1-932474-63-3

Special Thanks to:

Tim Yarbrough of Moulton, Alabama for urging me to read and reprint this little gem of a book.
Wayne Sparkman of the PCA Historical Center for his help in searching out biographical information about N.S. McFetridge.

Manufactured in the United States of America

Table of Contents

Introductory Essay

"What is Calvinism?"

By Benjamin B. Warfield

IT is very odd how difficult it seems for some persons to understand just what Calvinism is. And yet the matter itself presents no difficulty whatever. It is capable of being put into a single sentence; and that, on level to every religious man's comprehension. For Calvinism is just religion in its purity. We have only, therefore, to conceive of religion in its purity, and that is Calvinism.

In what attitude of mind and heart does religion come most fully to its rights? Is it not in the attitude of prayer? When we kneel before God, not with the body merely, but with the mind and heart, we have assumed the attitude which above all others deserves the name of religious. And this religious attitude by way of eminence is obviously just the attitude of utter dependence and humble trust. He who comes to God in prayer, comes not in a spirit of self-assertion, but in a spirit of trustful dependence. No one ever addressed God in prayer thus: "O God, thou knowest that I am the architect of my own fortunes and the determiner of my own destiny. Thou mayest indeed do something to help me in the securing of my purposes after I have determined upon them. But my heart is my own, and thou canst not intrude into it; my will is my own, and thou canst not bend it. When I wish thy aid, I will call on thee for it. Meanwhile, thou must await my pleasure." Men may reason somewhat like this; but that is not the way they pray. There did, indeed, once two men go up into the temple to pray. And one stood and prayed thus to himself (can it be that this "to himself" has a deeper significance than appears on the surface?), "God, I thank thee that I am not as the rest of men." While the other smote his breast, and said, "God be merciful to me a sinner." Even the former acknowledged a certain dependence on God; for he thanked God for his virtues. But we are not left in doubt in which one the religious mood was most purely exhibited. There is One who has told us that with clearness and emphasis.

All men assume the religious attitude, then, when they pray. But many men box up, as it were, this attitude in their prayer, and shutting it off from their lives with the Amen, rise from their knees to assume a totally different attitude, if not of heart, then at least of mind. They pray as if they were dependent on God's mercy alone; they reason—perhaps they even live—as if God, in some of his activities at least, were dependent on them. The Calvinist is the man who is determined to preserve the attitude he takes in prayer in all his thinking, in all his feeling, in all his doing. That is to say, he is the man who is determined that religion in its purity shall come to its full rights in his thinking, and feeling, and living. This is the ground of his special mode of thought, by reason of which he is called a Calvinist; and as well of his special mode of acting in the world, by reason of which he has become the greatest regenerating force in the world. Other men are Calvinists on their knees; the Calvinist is the man who is determined that his intellect, and heart, and will shall remain on their knees continually, and only from this attitude think, and feel, and act. Calvinism is, therefore, that type of thought in which there comes to its rights the truly religious attitude of utter dependence on God and humble trust in his mercy alone for salvation.

There are at bottom but two types of religious thought in the world—if we may improperly use the term "religious" for both of them. There is the religion of faith; there is the "religion" of works. Calvinism is the pure embodiment of the former of these; what is known in Church History as Pelagianism is the pure embodiment of the latter of them. All other forms of "religious" teaching which have been known in Christendom are but unstable attempts at compromise between the two. At the opening of the fifth century, the two fundamental types came into direct conflict in remarkably pure form as embodied in the two persons of Augustine and Pelagius. Both were expending themselves in seeking to better the lives of men. But Pelagius in his exhortations threw men back on themselves; they were able, he declared, to do all that God demanded of them—otherwise God would not have demanded it. Augustine on the contrary pointed them in their weakness to God; "He himself," he said, in his pregnant speech, "He himself is our power." The one is the "religion" of proud self-dependence; the other is the religion of dependence on God. The one is the "religion" of works; the other is the religion of faith. The one is not "religion" at all—it is mere moralism; the other is all that is in the world that deserves to be called religion. Just in proportion as this attitude of faith is present in our thought, feeling, life, are we religious. When it becomes regnant in our thought, feeling, life, then are we truly religious. Calvinism is that type of thinking in which it has become regnant.

"There is a state of mind," says Professor William James in his lectures on *The Varieties of Religious Experience*, "known to religious men, but to no others, in which the will to assert ourselves and hold our own has been displaced by a willingness to close our mouths and be as nothing in the floods and waterspouts of God." He is describing what he looks upon as the truly religious mood

3

as over against what he calls "mere moralism." "The moralist," he tells us, "must hold his breath and keep his muscles tense;" and things go well with him only when he can do so. The religious man, on the contrary, finds his consolation in his very powerlessness; his trust is not in himself, but in his God; and "the hour of his moral death turns into his spiritual birthday." The psychological analyst has caught the exact distinction between moralism and religion. It is the distinction between trust in ourselves and trust in God. And when trust in ourselves is driven entirely out, and trust in God comes in, in its purity, we have Calvinism. Under the name of religion at its height, what Professor James has really described is therefore just Calvinism.

We may take Professor James' testimony, therefore, as testimony that religion at its height is just Calvinism. There are many forms of religious teaching in the world which are not Calvinism. Because, teaching even in religion often (ordinarily even) offers us only "broken lights." There is no true religion in the world, however, which is not Calvinistic—Calvinistic in its essence, Calvinistic in its implications. When these implications are soundly drawn out and stated, and the essence thus comes to its rights, we obtain just Calvinism. In proportion as we are religious, in that proportion, then, are we Calvinistic; and when religion comes fully to its rights in our thinking, and feeling, and doing, then shall we be truly Calvinistic. This is why those who have caught a glimpse of these things, love with passion what men call "Calvinism," sometimes with an air of contempt; and why they cling to it with enthusiasm. It is not merely the hope of true religion in the world: it is true religion in the world—as far as true religion is in the world at all.

4

Author's Preface

THIS little book is made up of six lectures which were delivered in the Wakefield Presbyterian Church, Germantown, Pennsylvania, and of whose publication I had, at the time, no thought. The Lectures were the result of my leisure reading on the subject during several years of a busy pastorate. On leaving the theological school at Allegheny, I hardly knew whether I was a Calvinist or an Arminian, or a nameless compound of both, although I had the benefit of Dr. A.A. Hodge's matchless teaching, which I now regard as one of the greatest blessings on my life. In that very uncomfortable—yet very natural—state of mind I set myself to a course of reading, doctrinal and historical, as opportunity offered. One of the results of that reading was these Lectures. My main object in these discourses was to look into the workings of the system of doctrines called "Calvinistic," and by its effects upon those who most heartily adopted it to form some estimate of its character. Therefore it is that I have brought forward the testimony of a large number of accepted authorities, many of whom are not Calvinists, and consequently not prejudiced in favor of Calvinism.

One difficulty with which I constantly met in writing these Lectures was that of getting so large a subject within limits so narrow. And although I have gone over the ground enthusiastically, I have endeavored to examine the subject *honestly,* my own peculiar state of mind precluding all controversial designs. Certainly, I can say that not one unfair statement has been intended; and I trust that the cast of the language employed will not lead anyone to infer the opposite.

Hoping, then, that this little book, which to me has been a laboring of love, will be of some use, and that it may speak a word in favor of a system of doctrine which, however regarded, is based on the truths of God's word and the facts of human experience, I send it forth into the great world of letters.

N.S. McFetridge

Germantown, Philadelphia, PA
January 2, 1882

Calvinism
As a Political Force

I

Calvinism
As a Political Force

THERE is nothing which so constantly controls the mind of man, and so intensely affects his character, as the views which he entertains of the Deity. These take up their abode in the inmost sanctuary of the heart, and give tone to all its powers and coloring to all its actions. Whatever the forms and activities of the outward life, as a man "thinketh in his heart, so is he." Men do, undoubtedly, liken God, in a measure, to themselves, and transfer to him somewhat of their own passions and predominating moral qualities, and determine the choice of their religion by the prevailing sentiments of their hearts and the habits in which they have been trained;[1] but it is also true that their conceptions of God have a controlling influence in forming their character and regulating their conduct. The unfaithful servant in the parable of the Talents gave as the reason for his idleness his conception of his master as a hard and exacting man. He shaped his conduct not by what his master was, but by what he believed him to be. And if that divine parable has a world-wide application, it

---

[1] See James McCosh, *The Method of Divine Government,* p. 463

9

discloses the secret spring of a man's life in the conceptions which he has of God. As these are true or false, so his character and life will be. "As long as we look upon God as an exactor, not a giver, exactors, and not givers, shall we be." "All the value of service rendered," says Dr. Arnot, "By intellectual and mortal beings depends on the thoughts of God which they entertain." Hence no sincerity of purpose and no intensity of zeal can atone for a false creed or save a man from the fatal consequences of wrong principles.

There can be, therefore, no better criterion of the character of a man's belief than the effects which that belief produces. "Grapes do not grow on bramble-bushes. Illustrious natures do not form themselves on narrow and cruel theories...The practical effect of a belief is the real test of its soundness. Where we find a heroic life appearing as the uniform fruits of a particular mode of opinion, it is childish to argue in the face of fact that the result ought to have been different."[2] "A bad tree cannot bring forth good fruit." It is by this test that I would now subject Calvinism to a brief historical criticism. Let its works witness to it, and be its justification or condemnation.

What, then, do we mean by Calvinism? It is foreign to my purpose to enter into any minute detail of the distinctive doctrines of Calvinism or to give in any way a controversial cast to these Lectures; for while I believe Calvinism to be the system of doctrine set forth in the word and works of God, and therefore most favorable to all godliness, I am free cordially to allow to all who differ from us the right of private judgment, and sincerely to rejoice in all that they are able to accomplish for the well-being of men and the glory of God. It is the right and privilege of every man and of every body of men to give a

---

[2] James A. Froude, *Calvinism,* p. 8.

reason for the hope that is in them, and to maintain by all lawful means what they conceive to be the truth. Intolerance is no part of our creed, unless it is the intolerance of all shams and lies and hypocrisies. Of such things we all are, I trust, intolerant. But as regards the sacred rights and privileges of men, Calvinism is one of the most tolerant and liberal of all systems of belief. Its adherents are ever found ready to recognize the brotherhood and equality of all evangelical churches, and to unite with them in all liberal ideas and Christian enterprises.

What, then, do we mean by Calvinism? I will let one answer who has gained the right to answer, and than whom no one is better qualified to answer—the Rev. Dr. Archibald Alexander Hodge.

He says: "'Calvinism' is a term used to designate, not the opinions of an individual, but a mode of religious thought or a system of religious doctrines of which the person whose name it bears was an eminent expounder. There have been from the beginning only three generically distinct systems of doctrine, or modes of conceiving and adjusting the facts and principles understood to be revealed in the Scriptures: the Pelagian, which denies the guilt, corruption and moral impotence of man, and makes him independent of the supernatural assistance of God. At the opposite pole is the Calvinistic, which emphasizes the guilt and moral impotence of man, exalts the justice and sovereignty of God, and refers salvation absolutely to the undeserved favor and new creative energy of God. Between these comes the manifold and elastic system of compromise once known as Semi-Pelagianism, and in modern times as Arminianism, which admits man's original corruption, but denies his guilt; regards redemption as a compensation for innate, and consequently irresponsible, disabilities; and refers the moral restoration of the individual to the co-operation of

11

the human with the divine energy, the determining factor
being the human will."[3]

We have here, in succinct form, an accurate definition
of the two systems of theology which are in active
operation today, and which, Dr. Pusey says, "are now, and
probably for the last time, in conflict"[4] —Calvinism and
Arminianism, the former taking its name from John
Calvin, a Frenchman, born in 1519, and the latter taking
its name from James Herman or (in Latin dress) Arminius,
a Dutchman, born in 1560. These men did not originate
the systems of doctrine which bear their names, but only
expounded them more fully and developed them into a
more perfect form. The same views were maintained at
least as early as the fourth century, when Augustine and
Pelagius stood in much the same attitude to each other as
Calvin and Arminius in the sixteenth century. Hence
Calvinism is frequently and correctly called Augustin-
ianism; and Arminianism, Semi-Pelagianism. These are
the two systems which are now most extensively held, and
with the one or the other of them all other Christian theological systems have organic sympathies.

Out of Arianism grew Socinianism, and out of that
modern Unitarianism, which makes Christ neither a man
nor God, but a created being somewhere above angels and
between humanity and Deity.[5] And while Arminianism is
neither Arian nor Socinian nor Unitarian, these all are
Arminian. As the writer of the article "Arminianism" in
the *American Cyclopedia* says, "Every new phase of
Arianism, to this day, is infallibly Arminian, though the
organic connection of the two is not so manifest from the
distinctively Arminian side, at least in modern times."

---

[3] Johnson's *Cyclopedia* article "Calvinism."
[4] His *Letter to the Archbishop of Canterbury*
[5] See Channing's *Works*, and Joseph Cook's exposition of them in *The Independent*, March, 1880.

Their organic connection might be easily traced, and their natural affinity easily shown, did it come within our present purpose. But there are other connections and affinities of these doctrines which demand our present consideration. Each of these two systems, Calvinism and Arminianism, has an organic connection and a natural affinity with a distinct form of church government—the Calvinistic with the presbyterial and independent form, and the Arminian with the prelatical or episcopal form. As a matter of fact, this has always been so. The Roman Episcopal Church has always been, as a Church, Arminian in doctrine, although her Thirty-nine Articles of Faith are Calvinistic. I once asked a learned Episcopal rector how it came that while his Confession of Faith is Calvinistic his Church is Arminian. Smiling, he replied, "The Calvinism in the Articles is so weak that you could drive a horse and cart through it at some points." That, I presume, accounts for it. It is not strong enough to hold the Church up to it or to resist the powerful tendency of Episcopacy to Arminian doctrines. The Methodist Episcopal Church also is, as a Church, Arminian. The fact, then, is that Arminianism and Episcopacy do naturally sympathize and affiliate. There is that in the Arminian doctrines of emotions and works which lead directly to the external forms and ceremonies of Prelacy or Episcopacy.

On the other hand, the Reformed churches which took the Presbyterian form of government have always been Calvinistic. As the Rev. Albert Barnes says, "There are no permanent Arminian, Pelagian, or Socinian presbyteries, synods, general assemblies on earth. There are no permanent instances where these forms of belief or unbelief take on the presbyterian forms of ecclesiastical administration where they would be long retained."[6]

---

[6] As quoted by Breed, *Presbyterianism Three Hundred years Ago,* p. 11.

13

This connection between the *doctrine* and the *form of worship is* not superficial or accidental, but inherent. A system of doctrine, as Pelagianism, which teaches salvation by our own good works or, as Arminianism, which teaches salvation partly by works and partly by grace, of necessity sympathizes and affiliates with rites and ceremonies, and lays, in the very spirit of it, the foundation for a ritualistic service. Romanism, which is rigid Arminianism, and Presbyterianism, which is strict Calvinism are the very antipodes of each other, and have always been in the most uncompromising hostility. Hence the historical fact that the higher the "Churchman" the more intensely Arminian he is. "It is a conspicuous fact of English history," says Dr. Hodge, "that high views as to the prerogatives of the ministry have always antagonized Calvinistic doctrines."[7] Hence also the simple republican form of worship in the Calvinistic churches.

Henry Thomas Buckle, who, himself a fatalist, cannot be charged with partiality toward any Church, says: "It is an interesting fact that the doctrines which in England are called Calvinistic have always been connected with a democratic spirit, while those of Arminianism have found most favor among the aristocratic or protective party. In the republics of Switzerland, of North America and of Holland, Calvinism was always the popular creed. On the other hand, in those evil days immediately after the death of Elizabeth, when our liberties were in imminent peril, when the Church of England, aided by the Crown, attempted to subjugate the consciences of men, and when the monstrous claim of the divine right of Episcopacy was first put forward,—then it was that Arminianism became the cherished doctrine of the ablest and most ambitious of the ecclesiastical party. And in that sharp retribution which followed, the Puritans and Independents, by whom

---

[7] Johnson's *Cyclopedia*, article, "Calvinism."

the punishment was inflicted, were, with scarcely an exception, Calvinists; nor should we forget that the first open movement against Charles proceeded from Scotland where the principles of Calvin had long been in the ascendant."[8]

Thus we see how Arminianism, taking to an aristocratic form of church government, tends toward monarchy in civil affairs, while Calvinism, taking to republican form of church government, tends toward democracy in civil affairs.

Allow me to quote again from this eminent English author. He says: "the first circumstance by which we must be struck is, that Calvinism is a doctrine for the poor and Arminianism for the rich. A creed which insists upon the necessity of faith must be less costly than one which insists upon the necessity of works. In the former case the sinner seeks salvation by the strength of his belief; in the latter case he seeks it by the fullness of his contributions" . . . "This is the first great practical divergence of the two creeds." . . . . "It is also observable that the Church of Rome, whose worship is addressed mainly to the senses, and which delights in splendid cathedrals and pompous ceremonies, has always displayed against the Calvinists an animosity far greater than she has done against any other Protestant sect." Continuing in this strain, he observes what he calls "the aristocratic tendency of Arminianism and the democratic tendency of Calvinism" and says: "The more any society tends to equality, the more likely it is that its theological opinions will be Calvinistic; while the more a society tends toward inequality, the greater the probability of those opinions being Arminian."[9]

These views of this writer are abundantly confirmed by the history bearing upon the subject. The historical fact

---

[8] *History of Civilization,* i. 611.
[9] *History of English Civilization,* i. pp. 612, 613.

is that Arminianism tends to beget and to foster classes and castes in society, and to build up a gorgeous ritual wherever it gains a foothold. And so it comes to be true, on the other hand, what the historian George Bancroft observes, that "a richly-endowed Church always leads to Arminianism and justification by works."[10]

Now let us glance at the explanation of this historical fact. The prelatical or episcopal form of church government, which has always been connected with Arminian doctrines, asserts that all church power is vested in the clergy; while the republican form, which has always accompanied Calvinistic doctrines, asserts that all church power is vested in the Church; that is, in the people. This is a radical difference, and "touches the very essence of things." If all the power be in the clergy, then the people are practically bound to passive obedience in all matters of faith and practice. Thus the one system subjects the people to the autocratic orders of a superior, the centre principle of monarchy and despotism; while the other system elevates the people to an equality in authority, the centre principle of democracy.

On this point I will quote a few sentences from the late Dr. Charles Hodge. "The theory," he observes, "that all church power vests in a divinely-constituted hierarchy begets the theory that all civil power vests, of divine right, in kings and nobles. And the theory that church power vests in the Church itself, and all church officers are servants of the Church, of necessity begets the theory that civil power vests in the people, and that civil magistrates are servants of the people. These theories God has joined together, and no man can put them asunder. It was therefore by an infallible instinct that the unfortunate Charles of England said, 'No bishop, no king;' by which he meant that if there is no despotic power in the Church,

---

[10] *History of the United States*, ix. p. 503.

there can be no despotic power in the State, or if there be liberty in the Church, there will be liberty in the State."[11]

We find, then, these three propositions proved by historical fact and logical sequence: First, Arminianism associates itself with an episcopal form of church government, and Calvinism with a republican form of church government; second, Episcopacy fosters ideas of inequality in society and of monarchy and one-man power in civil affairs; and, third, Arminianism is unfavorable to civil liberty, and Calvinism is unfavorable to despotism. The despotic rulers of former days were not slow to observe the correctness of these propositions, and, claiming the divine right of kings, feared Calvinism as republicanism itself.

Now, consider, for a moment, some of the reasons which lie in the system of Calvinism for its strong hostility to all despotism and its powerful influence in favor of civil liberty.

One reason for this may be found in the boundary-line which it draws between Church and State. It gives to each its distinct sphere, and demands that the one shall not assume the prerogatives of the other. In this it differs from Lutheranism, "which soon settled down at peace with princes, while Calvinism was ever advancing and ever contending with rulers of the world;"[12] and from the Anglican system, which began with Henry VIII as its head in place of the pope. This distinction between Church and State is, as the eminent Yale professor, Dr. George P. Fisher, remarks, "the first step, the necessary condition, in the development of religious liberty without which civil liberty is an impossibility."[13]

---

[11] *What is Presbyterianism? p.* 11.
[12] Dr. Henry B. Smith, *Faith and Philosophy.*
[13] *History of the Reformation.*

Another reason is found in the republican character of its polity. Its clergy are on a perfect equality. No one of them stands higher in authority than another. They are all alike bishops. Its laymen share equally with its clergymen in all official acts—in the discussion and decision of all matters of doctrine and practice. They have a most important part given them in the right of choosing and calling their own pastor. By being thus rulers in the Church they are taught to claim an exercise the same liberty in the State. It is this feature of the Calvinistic system which has, from the first, exalted the layman. It constitutes, not the clergy, but the Christian people, the interpreter of the divine will. To it the voice of the majority is the voice of God, and the issue, therefore, is, as Bancroft observes, "popular sovereignty."[14]

Another reason why Calvinism is favorable to liberty lies in its theology. "The sense of the exaltation of the Almighty Ruler," says Dr. Fisher, "and of his intimate connection with the minutest incidents and obligations of human life, which is fostered by this theology dwarfs all earthly potentates. An intense spirituality, consciousness that this life is but an infinitesimal fraction of human existence, dissipates the feeling of personal homage for men, however high their station, and dulls the luster of all earthly grandeur". . . . "The Calvinist, unlike the Romanist, dispenses with a human priesthood, which has not only often proved a powerful direct auxiliary to temporal rulers, but has *educated the sentiments to a habit of subjection,* which renders submission to such rulers more facile and less easy to shake off."[15]

Its doctrine of predestination also is calculated to have a tremendous influence on the political character of its adherents. This has not escaped the notice of historians.

---

[14] *History of the United States,* i. pp. 44, 461.
[15] See Fisher's *History of the Reformation.*

Bancroft, who, while adopting another religious creed, has awarded to Calvinism the palm for its influence in favor of religious and civil liberty, remarks that "the political character of Calvinism, which, with one consent and with instinctive judgment, the monarchs of that day feared as republicanism, is expressed in a single word— *predestination.* Did a proud aristocracy trace its lineage through generations of a highborn ancestry, the republican Reformers, with a loftier pride, invaded the invisible world, and from the book of life brought down the record of the noblest enfranchisement, decreed from eternity by the King of kings . . . They went forth in confidence, . . . and, standing surely amidst the crumbling fabric of centuries of superstition, they had faith in one another; and the martyrdoms of Cambray, the fires of Smithfield, the surrender of benefices by two thousand non-conforming Presbyterians, attests their perseverance."[16]

This doctrine "inspires a resolute, almost defiant, freedom in those who deem themselves the subjects of God's electing grace; in all things they are more than conquerors through the confidence that nothing shall be able to separate them from the love of God. No doctrine of the dignity of human nature, of the rights of man, of national liberty, of social equality, can create such a resolve for the freedom of the soul as this personal conviction of God's favoring and protecting sovereignty. He who has this faith feels that he is compassed about with everlasting love, guided with everlasting strength; his will is the tempered steel that no fire can melt, no force can break. Such faith is freedom; and this spiritual freedom is the source and strength of all other freedom."[17]

Having thus briefly traced the spirit and tendency of Calvinism in relation to liberty, I will now indicate, from

---

[16] *History of the United States,* vol. ii, p. 461.
[17] *The United States as a Nation,* p. 30, by Rev. Joseph Thompson, D.D.

the testimony of those most capable of giving impartial judgment, what Calvinism has *done for civil liberty.*

And here let it be remarked that events follow principles; that mind rules the world; that thought is more powerful than cannon; that "all history is in its inmost nature religious;"[18] and that, as John von Muller says, "Christ is the key to the history of the world," and, as Carlyle says, "the spiritual will always body itself forth in the temporal history of men." In the formation of the modern nations religion performed a principal part. The great movements out of which the present civilized nations sprung were religious through and through.

What part, then, had Calvinism in begetting and shaping and controlling those movements? What has it to show as the result of its labors? A rich possession indeed. A glorious record belongs to it in the history of modern civilization.

Be it remembered that Luther was an Augustinian or Calvinistic monk, and that it was from this rigorous theology that he learned the great truth, the pivot of the Reformation and the kindling flame of civilization— salvation, not by works, but *by faith alone.* True, indeed, that truth was first laid down in the word of God. We can accept as complimentary the sneering remark of Ernest Renan, that Paul begat Augustine, and Augustine begat Calvin, and Calvin begat the Jansenists and their brethren. We glory in the lineal decent. And we stand willing also to acknowledge the kindness of Matthew Arnold, when, in his vain attempts to cut Calvinism out of the New Testament and fling it away, he declares Paul to have been the author of it, but excuses the great apostle for being guilty of it by saying that he allowed himself "to fall into it" through mistake and through the speculative bent of his

---

[18] Dr. H.B. Smith's *Faith and Philosophy.*

intellect.[19] But one might be tempted to ask Mr. Arnold, how could Paul have "fallen into it" unless it had been already in existence? And from what ground did the great apostle fall? Truly the Church is in a sad plight if the doctrines of the apostles are the errors which they "fell into"! It is pleasing, however, to some of us to find such men as these attributing the paternity of Calvinism to St. Paul, and to find them driven to such extremities in their efforts to explain it away as to be compelled to say that Paul was mad, or, as an Arminian clergyman of our own city has said, that "Paul was not converted when he wrote the book of Romans."

So, then, enemies themselves being witness, Paul had laid down the grand truth which Luther found in his study of the Augustinian theology and of the Bible. The Arminianism of the Church of Rome had so perverted that truth, and so wrapped it over with its "works of righteousness," as to make it practically unknown. It was not till Luther had grasped it clearly and firmly in his intellect and heart that it became again a living thing and a mighty force. Henceforth the secret power and stirring watchword of the Reformation was *justification by faith alone*. It was this cleanly-cut and strong theology which began the Reformation, and which carried it on through fire and flood, through all opposition and terror and persecution and misery, to its glorious consummation. When in the great toil and roar of the conflict the fiery nature of Luther began to chill, and he began to temporize with civil rulers, it was this same uncompromising theology of the Genevan school which heroically and triumphantly waged the conflict to the end. I but repeat the testimony of history, friendly and unfriendly to Calvinism, when I say that had it not been for the strong, unflinching, systematic spirit and character of the theology of Calvin,

---

[19] Matthew Arnold, *St. Paul and Puritanism.*

the Reformation would have been lost to the world. That is one thing which Calvinism has done. That is one of the fruits which have grown on this vigorous old tree.

Hence it was that almost everywhere the Reformation assumed the Calvinistic type, supplanting or absorbing all other reforming ideas. Even in the lands, such as Germany and Switzerland, where the peculiarly Lutheran ideas had first found acceptance, it was "through the influence of Calvinistic principles that the Protestantism of those lands assumed an external form and organization, and attained to definite dimensions in the history of the world."[20] In this system only were found that vigor and that earnestness which are essential to the highest success. Even Luther himself, when the splendor of Calvin's name was outshining his own, withheld not his admiration and praise from the strict discipline which prevailed in the Calvinistic churches, and from that lofty earnestness which pervades the whole Calvinistic system of reform, and which gave it more and more of that steady consistency that was requisite in its conflict with opposing powers, and without which no victory is ever attained.[21]

"The Lutheran congregations were but half emancipated from superstition, and shrank from pressing the struggle to extremities; and half measures meant half-heartedness, convictions which were but half convictions, and truth with an alloy of falsehood. Half measures, however, would not quench the bonfires of Philip of Spain or raise men in France or Scotland who would meet crest to crest the princes of the house of Lorraine. The Reformers required a position more sharply defined and a sterner leader, and that leader they found in John Calvin. For hard times hard men are needed, and intellects which can pierce to the roots where truth and lies part company.

---

[20] Karl R. Hagenbach's *History of the Reformation*, vol. ii, p. 350.
[21] Hagenbach

It fares ill with the soldiers of religion when 'the accursed thing' is in the camp. And this is to be said of Calvin, that, so far as the state of knowledge permitted, no eye could have detected more keenly the unsound spots in the creed of the Church, nor was there a Reformer in Europe so resolute to exercise, tear out and destroy what was distinctly seen to be false—so resolute to establish what was true in its place, and make truth, to the last fibre of it, the rule of practical life."[22]

This is the testimony of a man who has no particular love for Calvinism, but who from the high ground of learned investigation looks at it and the man whose name it bears through the light of historical fact.

And in further explication of this thought allow me to quote again from the same authority: "Was it not written long ago, 'He that will save his soul shall lose it'? If we think of religion only as a means of escaping what we call the wrath to come, we shall not escape it; we are already under it; we are under the burden of death, for we care only for ourselves. This was not the religion of your fathers; this was not the Calvinism which overthrew spiritual wickedness, and hurled kings from their thrones, and purged England and Scotland, for a time at least, of lies and charlatanry. Calvinism was the spirit which rises in revolt against untruth—the spirit which, as I have shown you, has appeared and reappeared, and in due time will appear again unless God be a delusion and man be as the beasts that perish. For it is but the inflashing upon the conscience of the nature and origin of the laws by which mankind are governed—laws which exist whether we acknowledge them or whether we deny them, and will have their way, to our own weal or woe, according to the attitude in which we place ourselves toward them— inherent, like the laws of gravity, in the nature of things;

---

[22] Froude, *Calvinism*, p. 42.

not made by us, not to be altered by us, but to be discerned and obeyed by us at our everlasting peril."[23]

This was the Calvinism which flashed forth in the great Reforming days—the spirit which, when Romanists and despots claimed the right to burn all who differed from them, inspired men and women and youth to go forth, Bible and sword in hand, to the greatest daring, appealing for the justice of their cause and the victory of their arms to the Lord of hosts. This was the spirit which acted in those men "who attracted to their ranks almost every man in Western Europe who hated a lie;" who when they were crushed down rose again; who "abhorred all conscious mendacity, all impurity, all moral wrong of every kind, so far as they could recognize it;" who, though they did not utterly destroy Romanism, "drew its fangs, and forced it to abandon that detestable principle that it was entitled to murder those who dissented from it." This was the spirit out of which came, and by which was nourished, the religious and civil liberties of Christendom; of which Bancroft says, "More truly benevolent to the human race than Solon, more self-denying than Lycurgus, the genius of Calvin infused enduring elements into the institutions of Geneva, and made it for the modern world the impregnable fortress of popular liberty, the fertile seed-plot of democracy."[24]

That religious and civil liberty have an organic connection and a natural affinity is quite obvious. They hold together as root and branch. "By the side of every religion is to be found a political opinion connected with it by affinity. If the human mind be left to follow its own bent, it will regulate the temporal and spiritual institutions of society in a uniform manner, and man will endeavor, if I

---

[23] Froude, *Calvinism*, pp. 46,47.
[24] Bancroft's *Essays*.

24

may so speak, to harmonize earth with heaven."[25] But other influences may be powerful enough to interfere with this natural connection of the religious and political belief. The Romanist may choose to be a republican rather than a monarchist, because of the greater advantages which a republic confers, or because he finds himself in the midst of republican institutions which he cannot hope to alter; but when a man is free to follow his own inclinations, he will body forth his religion in his political beliefs. Hence it comes that the influence on our republican institutions of a rigid Arminianism, which has always been wedded to an aristocratic form of church government, is unfavorable to their perpetuity. Its whole tendency, politically, is to educate the sentiments of the people to a spirit of subjection to the rich and powerful, and thus to prepare them for the monarchic form of civil government.

Charles I of England gave as the reason why his father James I, had subverted the republican form of government of the Scottish Church, that the presbyterial and monarchical forms of government do not harmonize.[26] And De Tocqueville, admitting the same, calls Calvinism "a democratic and republican religion."[27] This is the historical fact, that, while Calvinism can live and do its divine work under any form of civil government, its natural affinities are not with a monarchy, but with a republic.

This is the reason that it has made so splendid a record in the history of human freedom. Where it flourishes despotism cannot abide. This, says the historian Merle D'Aubigne, "chiefly distinguishes the Reformation of Calvin from that of Luther, that wherever it was established it brought with it not only *truth*, but *liberty,* and all

---

[25] De Tocqueville, *Democracy*, i, p. 383.
[26] Buckle, ii, p. 206, note 5.
[27] *Democracy*, i., p. 384.

the great developments which these two fertile principles carry with them."[28]

Now, if we ask what Calvinism did for the cause of civil and religious liberty in France and the Netherlands, we have but to turn to the glowing pages of D'Aubigne and to the enchanting histories of our own Motley. It created, under God, the Dutch Republic, and made it "the first free nation to put a girdle of empire around the world." Account for it as one will, the fact is, that until Calvinism took possession of the Netherlanders and gained the ascendancy over all other religious beliefs, the people made but little headway against the powerful empire of Spain; but from that moment they never faltered for well nigh a hundred years, until their independence was triumphantly established. Their great leader, William the Silent, prince of Orange, was, as it would appear, forced logically, consistently and necessarily to give up first his Romanism and next his Lutheranism, and to become a sincere and rigid Calvinist while fighting for his country's independence. Then it was that he began to exhibit such vigor and enthusiasm and perseverance as he had never before exhibited. Then it was that he began to make those bleak fields of the North to be the light and hope of the Protestant world and the terror of the proud and powerful Philip of Spain. "It would certainly be unjust and futile," says Motley, "to detract from the vast debt which that republic owed to the Genevan Church. The Reformation had entered the Netherlands by the Walloon gate (that is, through the Calvinists). The earliest and most eloquent preachers, the most impassioned converts, the sublimest martyrs, had lived, preached, fought, suffered and died with the precepts of Calvin in their hearts. The fire which had consumed the last vestige of royal and sacerdotal despotism throughout the independent republic had been lighted by the hands of Calvinists."

[28] *History of the Reformation in the Time of Calvin*, vol. i, p. 3

26

"Throughout the blood-stained soil of France, too, the men who were fighting the same great battle as were the Netherlanders against Philip II and the Inquisition, the valiant cavaliers of Dauphiny and Provence, knelt on the ground before the battle, smote their iron breasts with their mailed hands, uttered a Calvinistic prayer, sang a psalm of Marot, and then charged upon Guise or upon Joyeuse under the white plume of the Bearnese. And it was on the Calvinistic weavers and clothiers of Rochelle that the Great Prince relied in the hour of danger, as much as on his mounted chivalry. In England, too, the seeds of liberty, wrapped up in Calvinism and hounded through many trying years, were at last destined to float over land and sea, and to bear largest harvests of temperate freedom for great commonwealths that were still unborn."[29] To the Calvinists, "more than to any other class of men, the political liberties of Holland, England and America are due."[30]

Such language might be mistaken for a mere panegyric of an intense Calvinist, did we not know that it is the historical testimony of one who was not a Calvinist, but who, with the fire of freedom burning brightly in his heart, and with a perfect knowledge of what he is saying, pays such lofty tributes to men who dared maintain the cause of liberty in the earth. This is sufficient to indicate, as I here can only do, what was the influence and what the worth of Calvinism on the liberties of France and the Netherlands.

Now let us cross the English Channel and see what Calvinism was as a political force on the green soil of England and on the heathered hills of Scotland.

It will be borne in mind that we make no such absurd claim as that *everyone* who fought for religious and civil

---

[29] John L. Motley, *The History of the Netherlands*, vol. iii, pp. 120,121.
[30] Ibid., vol. iv, p. 547.

liberty in those days was a Calvinist. We claim only that almost all of them were Calvinists and that their great leaders were Calvinists. This is the historical fact, that it was the Calvinists who did the reforming work, rough and sore as it was, in England, Ireland and Scotland. Henry VIII only *transformed* the Church; he did not *reform* it. The Anglican Church was established not from the convictions of the people, but by the decree of the king, who became its supreme pontiff. I would not care to say what Alphonse of Lamartine says about the laying of its foundations, lest I might be taken as uncharitable toward a Church which I greatly venerate, excepting only that wherein she has been unfaithful to herself and to Protestantism in her High-Churchism, by which she has given occasion to Romanists to call her "a bulwark against the aggressiveness of the non-conforming churches," and to plead for her continuance on that ground. But all understand how she came into existence— not by faith of the people, but by the will of the sovereign. Yet no royal decree can reform a Church or people. Reformation must be the work of the individual conscience. Hence, when the Anglican Church was suddenly cut away from Rome, and had become, as it were, "an English translation of the Latin," the real reforming work had still to be done. And who did it? Was it the Arminians? No; they had little or no hand in it. As Macaulay says, "The Lambeth Articles," which were drawn up by Elizabeth's favorite bishop in concert with the bishop of London and other theologians, "affirm the Calvinistic doctrines with a distinctness which would shock many who in our age are reputed Calvinists." "Arminianism," he continues, "with its more popular notions, came in later."[31] Through all the struggles of those two centuries it was the Calvinists who were always contending, sometimes badly and bitterly enough, but ever

---

[31] *The History of England*, vol. i, p. 23.

28

honestly and earnestly, for the heavenly boon of human freedom. It was they who reformed Scotland, and lifted her out of the pit of darkness and misery in which she had been so long confined.

The spirit in which they carried on the conflict is well illustrated in the case of Jennie Geddes. Charles I had determined to carry out his father's policy of compelling the Scotch Church to adopt Prelacy. The city of Edinburgh and the church of St. Giles was the place the public use of the Liturgy was to be commenced. The church was crowded, and "a deep, melancholy calm brooded over the congregation," presaging the fierce tempest which was about to sweep away every barrier. At length the dean, attired in his surplice, began to read the Liturgy, but his voice was speedily drowned in tumultuous clamor. An old woman, Jennie Geddes, was the heroine of the occasion. "Villain!" she cried, "doest thou say mass at my lug?"[32] and with that she hurled the stool on which she had been sitting at the dean's head. Others quickly followed her example, and compelled the dean to fly, leaving his surplice behind him. This was really the death-blow to the Liturgy in Scotland,[33] and it exhibits the earnest, fearless spirit of even the aged and humble.

But the one man who was the principal instrument in the hand of Providence in reforming Scotland was John Knox. He had learned his theology at the feet of Calvin in Geneva, and had known, as a galley-slave, the tender mercies of Romanism. He was one of the six clerical Johns who composed the first General Assembly of Scotland. Now, let us take the testimony of history as to the worth of this man. Thus Froude speaks: "John Knox, to whose teaching they (the Scotch) owed their *national existence.*" . . . "Such was Knox, the greatest of living Scotchmen." . .

[32] In old Scottish lug meant *the ear.*
[33] Dr. James G. Craighead's, *Irish Seeds in American Soil*, p. 80.

29

"No grander figure can be found in the entire history of the Reformation in this island than that of Knox. Cromwell and Burghley rank beside him for the work which they effected, but as politicians and statesmen they had to labor with instruments with which they soiled their hands in touching. In purity, in uprightness, in courage, truth and stainless honor the regent Murray and our English Latimer were perhaps his equals; but Murray was intellectually far below him, and the sphere of Latimer's influence was on small scale. The time has come when English history may do justice to one but for whom the *Reformation would have been overthrown* among ourselves; for the spirit which Knox created saved Scotland; and if Scotland had been Catholic again, neither the wisdom of Elizabeth's ministers, nor the teaching of her bishops, nor her own chicaneries, would have preserved England from revolution. His was the voice which taught the peasant of the Lothians that he was a free man, the equal in the sight of God with the proudest peer or prelate that had trampled on his forefathers. He was the one antagonist whom Mary Stuart could not soften nor Maitland deceive; he it was that raised the poor Commons of his country into a stern and rugged people, who might be hard, narrow, superstitious and fanatical, but who, nevertheless, were men whom neither king, noble nor priest could force again to submit to tyranny. And his reward has been the ingratitude of those who should most have done honor to his memory."[34]

Now, take another testimony to the worth and work of this man—that of the man of philosophical literature, Thomas Carlyle. Thus he speaks: "This that Knox did for his nation, I say, we may really call a resurrection as from death. It was not a smooth business; but it was welcome surely, and cheap at that price had it been far rougher. On

---

[34] *English History*, vol. x, p. 437.

the whole, cheap at any price;—as life is. The people began to live; they needed first of all to do that, at what cost and costs soever. Scotch literature and thought; Scotch industry; James Watt, David Hume, Walter Scott, Robert Burns,—I find Knox and the Reformation acting in the heart's core of every one of these persons and phenomena. It seems to me hard measure that this Scottish man, now after three hundred years, should have to plead like a culprit before the world, intrinsically for having been, in such a way as it was then possible to be, the bravest of all Scotch men. Had he been a poor half-and-half, he could have crouched into the corner, like so many others; Scotland had not been delivered; and Knox had been without blame. He is the one Scotchman to whom, of all others, his country and the world owe a debt." . . . "Honor to him! His works have not died. The letter of his works dies, as of all men's; but the spirit of it never!"

Such is the estimate of history upon Knox and his work after three hundred years, a period long enough for the judging of them correctly, and long enough to sink most men's works into oblivion. It was, however, unfortunate for the reputation of Knox with a certain class of people that he was compelled by truth and conscience and the welfare of his nation and Protestantism to oppose a woman, young, beautiful, bad and royal—Mary Stuart, queen of Scots; with whom to be a favorite it was necessary to be false to Scotland and to the Reformation, and whose troublous life and unfortunate death softened the heart of the world toward her, blinding many to her serious faults.

Other causes also have contributed to obscure his glory and to depreciate his real worth and the value of his services. He belonged to a Church which was unpopular at court, and which is not yet popular in royal residences. "On the other hand," Buckle says, "the sect of Episcopalians in Scotland are utterly blind to the real

31

grandeur of the man, and unable to discern his intense love of truth and the noble fearlessness of his nature."[35]

In addition to these causes, Knox has had no competent biographer. The bard in ancient times was necessary to the hero's fame; so is the historian in these latter days. Knox's bard is yet to come; and he will come.

As to what the Calvinists did in Scotland during those trying and important times toward the close of the sixteenth century, we must content ourselves with quoting a few sentences from Buckle's *History of Civilization in England*: "In their pulpits, in their presbyteries, and in their general assemblies they encouraged a democratic and insubordinate tone, which eventually produced the happiest results by keeping alive, at a critical moment, the spirit of liberty." . . . "Let us then, not be too rash in this matter. Let us not be too forward in censuring the leading actors in the great crisis through which Scotland passed during the latter half of the sixteenth century. Much they did which excites our strongest aversion. But one thing they achieved which should make us honor their memory and repute them benefactors of their species. At a most hazardous moment they kept alive the spirit of national liberty. What the nobles and the Crown had put in peril, that did the clergy save. By their care the dying spark was kindled into a blaze. When the light grew dim and flickered on the altar, their hands trimmed the lamp and fed the sacred flame. This is their real glory, and on this they may well repose. They were the guardians of Scotch freedom, and they stood to their post. Where danger was, they were foremost. By their sermons, by their conduct, both public and private, by the proceedings of their assemblies, by their bold and frequent attacks upon persons without regard to their rank—nay, even by the very insolence with which they treated their superiors—

---

[35] *History of Civilization*, vol. ii, p. 177, note.

they stirred up the minds of men, woke them from their lethargy, formed them to habits of discussion, and excited that inquisitive and democratic spirit which is the only effectual guarantee the people can ever possess against the tyranny of those who are set over them. This was the work of the Scotch clergy; and all hail to them who did it! To these men England and Scotland owe a debt they can never pay."[36]

These, then were some of the results achieved by the Calvinists in that great and sore struggle toward the close of the sixteenth century. But the struggle did not end with the century; it was continued for nearly a century afterward. When James I of England, son of Mary Stuart queen of Scots, ascended the throne in 1603, the conflict was renewed in earnest. Not caring particularly either for Episcopacy or Presbytery, excepting so far as he could use them for the furtherance and maintenance of his own despotic purposes, but believing Episcopacy to be the natural ally of the throne, and knowing from past experience that he could not bend the Presbyterians to his will, he devoted himself to the overthrow of the Presbyterian form of church government in Scotland, which had been established by Parliament. This arrayed against him a people who otherwise would have been loyal to their heart's core to the king who was their countryman, and who had repeatedly given his royal assurance that he would defend the liberties of his native land. By every power at his command he sought to impose upon the Scottish Church a form of government which was not only odious to her, but which she regarded as the shadow and symbol of Popery. By royal decree, by confiscation, by banishment, by a ruthless and relentless soldiery, by almost every cruel device, he used his great power to carry out the dictates of his imperial will and to silence every

---

[36] Vol. ii, pp. 185, 203, 204.

voice that was raised in defense of freedom and against his arbitrary and tyrannical measures.

This infamous work was carried on by his son and successor, Charles I, until the spirit of freedom, so long and mercilessly trampled upon, arose in its flaming wrath, and, led by Oliver Cromwell, himself a descendant of the royal house of Stuart through his mother, hurled the proud monarch from the throne and appeased its vengeance in his blood. When Cromwell, the great Calvinistic leader and commoner and Protector, was borne to his grave, after having formed the finest army that Europe had ever seen, and made the name of England terrible to every nation on the face of he earth,[37] and when his son, without his father's ability, retired from the government of the nation to which he had been called, preferring the ease of a country gentleman to the troublous position of a Lord Protector, the English people welcomed with much enthusiasm, and yet with great fear, another royal son to the throne in the person of Charles II, whose name and reign are amongst the most infamous in the annals of English history. If his predecessors had chastised the people with whips, he chastised them with scorpions. Unwisely neglecting his father's dying counsel, to forgive his enemies; he made the distress and cry of his independent subjects sore against him. In this he was imitated by his successor, James II, the abject pensioner of Louis XIV of France.

During these reigns the Calvinists, and especially they of Scotland, were subjected to a tyranny so cruel and exhausting as might have crushed out for ever the energy of almost any people. Corrupt and ignorant judges sat upon the bench to issue decrees in accordance with the wish of the monarch, and miserable slaves of men pretty largely made up the Parliaments. England and Scotland

---

[37] Lord Macaulay, *"Essays on Milton."*

have seen no darker days in all their history. History is compelled to confess, though she do it with confused face and profound sorrow, that amongst the most zealous alders and abettors of these despotic sovereigns were the bishops and clergy of the Anglican Church. That such men as William Laud, archbishop of Canterbury, and James Sharp, a renegade Presbyterian, archbishop of St. Andrews, and John Leslie, bishop of Raphoe, Ireland, should have worn the robes of ecclesiastical authority, representing the rule of our Lord and Savior on the earth, is enough to fill any Christian heart with grief, and to cause the Church to which they belonged to seek to blot out her history for well nigh a hundred years, and to silence, until the judgment-day, her absurd and uncharitable claims to an apostolic succession. History cannot forget that many of the bishops of that day openly favored, and often suggested, the atrocities that were committed, and that when constitutional liberty and all the rights dearest to men who have the Anglo-Saxon blood in their veins, and who speak the English tongue, were struggling for an existence on earth, they presented James II with an address in which they called him "the darling of Heaven," and prayed that "God would give him the hearts of his subjects and the necks of his enemies."[38] "We ought never to forget," says an eminent English writer, "that the first and only time the Church of England has made war upon the Crown was when the Crown had declared its intention of tolerating, and in some degree protecting, the rival religions of the country."[39] Let it be borne in mind, however, that many of the bishops and archbishops of those times were consecrated to their offices neither by God nor the Church, but by the reigning sovereign. In Ireland alone, among all the numerous clergy of the

[38] Malcolm Laing's *History of Scotland*, vol. iv, p. 193.
[39] Buckle, vol. i, p. 288.

35

Church In the reign of Charles II., there were not a hundred of them episcopally ordained.[40]

Who, then, sustained the cause of liberty in those sore and protracted days? Who but the Calvinists, known as the Puritans, the Covenanters, the Round-heads, the Presbyterians, the Independents? When the people were abandoned to the lawless fury and wrath of their rulers, when they were ruthlessly plundered, murdered, and hunted like wild beasts from place to place, the Presbyterian clergy never deserted them: for five-and-eighty years that clergy never wavered but were always steady to the good cause and always on the side of the people.[41]

Of Cromwell and his work Carlyle says: "Indisputably, this too was a Heroism and the soul of it remains a part of the eternal soul of things. Here, of our own land and lineage, in practical English shape, were heroes on the earth once more; who knew in every fibre, and with heroic daring laid to heart, that an Almighty justice does verily rule this world; and that it is good to fight on God's side, and bad to fight on the devil's side; the essence of all heroisms and verities that have been or that will be. Perhaps it was among the nobler, and noblest human heroisms, this Puritanism of ours."[42]

Thrice was the crown of England offered to Cromwell, and pressed upon him, but he as often refused to accept it. As Lamartine says, "he ruled as a patriot, who only thought of the greatness and power of his country." And his rule "added more strength and prosperity to England than the nation had ever experienced under her most illustrious monarchs."[43]

---

[40] Craighead, *Scotch and Irish Seeds*, p. 226.
[41] Buckle, vol. ii, pp. 261, 262.
[42] *Cromwell's Letters*, vol. I, p. 8, Edinburgh edition.
[43] Lamartine's *Cromwell*.

If we ask again, who brought the final great deliverance to English liberty? we are answered by history, the illustrious Calvinist, William, prince of Orange, who as Macaulay says, found in the strong and sharp logic of the Genevan school something that suited his intellect and his temper; the keystone of whose religion was the doctrine of predestination; and who, with his keen logical vision declared that if he were to abandon the doctrine of predestination he must abandon with it all his belief in a superintending Providence, and must become a mere Epicurean.[44] And he was right, for predestination and an overruling Providence are one and the same thing. If we accept the one, we are in consistency bound to accept the other.

It was the battle of the Boyne (in Ireland, 1690) that decided the fate of Protestantism, not only for Great Britain, but for America; and for the world indeed, for had William been defeated there, Protestants could not have found a safe shelter on the face of the earth. "Orangemen" may therefore be pardoned for their lively interest in that battle.

On one side was James II, whom the poet Wordsworth appropriately calls, "The vacillating bond-man of the pope," with an army composed of his Roman Catholic and sympathizing subjects and allies. On the other side was his son-in-law, William, whom the Protestants had called from Holland to their deliverance—a little, but not a small man; pale and sickly; the world-acknowledged representative of the reforming cause; with an army much inferior in numbers to that of his royal father-in-law and opponent, but bound together as one man by a common faith and a glorious purpose. The world has never seen such another army. The entire Calvinistic world was represented in it.

---

[44] *History of England*, vol. ii, p. 49.

Less than four years before (October 22, 1685) Louis
XIV of France had published the Revocation of the Edict
of Nantes, by which all the rights and privileges of his
Calvinistic subjects, the Huguenots, were swept away.
This drove thousands upon thousands of them to flee from
their native land and to seek safety and liberty in other
climes. Multitudes of them had fled to William in Holland,
many of whom were of the best sailors and soldiers of
France. This seems indeed to have been a providence by
which William's army was to be reinforced and the great
victory to be won. Under him, at the Boyne, there were
Calvinists from England, Ireland, Scotland, France,
Prussia, Finland, Sweden and Switzerland, in addition to
his own staunch Hollanders and two hundred English
negro servants, as loyal to Christ and liberty as any under
the Orange flag. Hundreds of them were clad in the varied
and worn garments of private citizens, which they had
brought from their own distant homes.

The officer next in command to William was that
splendid military chieftain who, as commander-in-chief,
had many a time led the French army to victory—Marshal
Schomberg, a Huguenot refugee, now some seventy years
of age and into whose care the devoted wife of William
had committed her husband in his perilous yet glorious
undertaking. We can almost pardon James for all his
follies because he was the father of that Mary, the noble,
devoted, self-sacrificing Protestant wife of William, prince
of Orange. Marshal Schomberg it was who, with his
regiment of refugee countrymen, led the charge. Taking
his position at their head, and pointing with his sword
across the river to the army of James strongly entrenched
on the opposite bank; he uttered the thrilling words,
"Allons, mes antis! rappelez votre courage et vos

ressentiments! Voila vos *persecuteurs!"*[45] That was
enough to arouse in them all their fiery energies. The
memories of the past, their faith and their fatherland, were
the inspirations of the moment. With these words of their
brave old general and countryman ringing in their hearts,
they plunged into the river under a furious fire from their
enemies and, followed by all the army, soon gained the
opposite shore, wading in water to the armpits; and
wavered not until James and his army were utterly routed.

On these two great leaders, a Hollander and a
Frenchman, to the everlasting glory of their countries, the
liberties of the world were then, under God, depending—
the one, William, almost unable to sit on his gray horse
from physical weakness and loss of blood from an arm
disabled by a ball from the enemy; the other venerable
with years and honors, who there, in the Boyne waters,
gave his precious blood and noble life a sacrifice for the
welfare of mankind. When England forgets the part taken
by the French Huguenots in securing her liberties she will
cover herself with infamy. It might appear as if the
historian Macaulay would have her forget it; for, strange
to say, he passes it over in silence. Is it possible that he
would carry the English jealousy of the French to such a
length? Well and justly may Michelet protest against his
lordship's evidently designed neglect of his countrymen at
the Boyne, and remind England that "the army of William
was strong precisely in that Calvinistic element which
James repudiated in England."[46]

We see, then, what element fought the decisive battle
of Protestantism at the Boyne. The very watchword of
William's army was Westminster, the word which was
before, and has been ever since, stamped on the symbols
of the Calvinistic churches.

---

[45] "Let us go, my anti! Recall your courage and your resentments! Voila
your persecutors"
[46] *History of Louis XIV*, p. 418.

Of William himself it is no part of my plan to speak. Enough it will be here to quote the lines of Wordsworth regarding him:

> "Calm as an under-current, strong to draw
> Millions of waves into itself, and run,
> From sea to sea, impervious to the sun
> And ploughing storm, the spirit of Nassau
> Swerves not (how blest if by religious awe
> Swayed, and thereby enabled to contend
> With the wide world's commotions) - from its end
> Swerves not diverted by a casual law.
> Had moral action e'er a nobler scope?
> The hero comes to liberate, not defy:
> And, while he marches on with steadfast hope,
> Conqueror beloved! expected anxiously!
> The vacillating bondmaid of the pope
> Shrinks from the verdict of his steadfast eye."

As to the effect of William's victory and reign as William III of England, "the most successful and the most splendid recorded in the history of any country," Macaulay says, "It has been, of all revolutions, the most beneficent; the highest eulogy that can be pronounced upon it is this, that it was England's *best,* and that, for the authority of law, for the security of property, for the peace of our streets, for the happiness of our homes, our gratitude is due, under Him who raises and pulls down nations at his pleasure, to the Long Parliament, to the Convention and to William of Orange."[47] And David Hume's testimony to the worth of the Calvinistic Puritans is equally strong. "So absolute," he says, "was the authority of the Crown that the raucous spark of liberty had been kindled and was preserved by the Puritans alone, and it was to this sect that

---

[47] *History of England*, vol. ii, pp. 196, 197.

the English owe *the whole freedom of their constitution."⁴⁸* And H.A. Taine, referring to the Calvinists of
Great Britain, says: "These men are the true heroes of
England; they display, in high relief the original
characteristics and noblest features of England—practical
piety, the rule of conscience, manly resolution,
indomitable energy. They founded England, in spite of the
corruption of the Stuarts and the relaxation of modern
manners, by the exercise of duty, by the practice of justice,
by obstinate toil, by vindication of right, by resistance to
oppression, by the conquest of liberty, by the repression of
vice. They founded Scotland; they founded the United
States; at this day they are, by their descendants, founding
Australia and colonizing the world."⁴⁹

---

[48] *History of England*, vol. v, p. 134.
[49] *History of English Literature*, vol. ii, p. 472.

Calvinism
As a Political Force
In the History of the United States

II

Calvinism

As a Political Force
In the History of the United States

W E come now to one of the brightest pages of Calvinistic history, that which records the political influence
of the Calvinists in the formation of the American nation. I
need not dwell on Calvinism in the colonies prior to the
struggle with the mother-country for independence. It is
enough to bear in mind that the Puritans, who formed the
great bulk of the settlers of New England, were rigid
Calvinists, who had brought with them all their high
principles of civil liberty, and all their aversion to the
ceremonies and government of the Anglican Church, and
all their devotion to the doctrines of the great Reformers.

Let us come at once to the great Revolutionary conflict by which the colonies became a free and independent
nation. My proposition is this—a proposition which the
history clearly demonstrates: That this great American
nation, which stretches her vast and varied territory from
sea to sea, and from the bleak hills of the North to the
sunny plains of the South, was the purchase chiefly of the
Calvinists, and the inheritance which they bequeathed to
all liberty-loving people.

It would be almost impossible to give the merest outline of the influence of the Calvinists on the civil and religious liberties of this continent without seeming to be a mere Calvinistic eulogist; for the contestants in the great Revolutionary conflict were, so far as religious opinions prevailed, so generally Calvinistic on the one side and Arminian on the other as to leave the glory of the result almost entirely with the Calvinists. They who are best acquainted with the history will agree most readily with the historian, Merle D'Aubigne, when he says: "Calvin was the founder of the greatest of republics. The Pilgrims, who left their country in the reign of James I, and, landing on the barren soil of New England, founded populous and mighty colonies, were his sons, his direct and legitimate sons; and that American nation which we have seen growing so rapidly boasts as its father the humble Reformer on the shores of Lake Leman."[50]

There was no place on this continent where the political agitation which resulted in independence was so vigorously kept up as in the city of New York. The two leading parties of that city, in wealth and influence, in politics and religion, at that time, were the Livingstons and De Lanceys. The Livingstons were Presbyterians, and consequently flaming republicans or whigs, and were supported almost unanimously by the dissenters; the De Lanceys were Episcopalians, and staunch loyalists, or Tories, and were supported as unanimously by the Episcopalians.[51] Hence the religious beliefs and differences contributed very largely to inflame the spirit of the opposing parties and to sustain it throughout the conflict; for not then as now, it will be remembered, did such liberal and fraternal sentiments pervade the various denominations. It was a formative, trying period, when the

---

[50] *History of the Reformation in the Time of Calvin*, vol. i, p. 5.
[51] Thomas Jones's *History of New York*, vol. ii, p. 291.

heat of debate and contention was felt and exhibited by all parties.

The various bodies of dissenters, mainly Calvinists, which had settled in the colonies, had been driven away from their fatherland, not by the persecutions of the Romanist Church, but by the tyranny of British sovereigns and the intolerance of the Anglican Church. It is to be remembered that the settlement of New England was the result, not of the contest between the Reforming opinions and the authority of Rome, but, as Bancroft says, "of the implacable differences between Protestant dissenters and the established Anglican Church . . . A young French refugee (John Calvin) skilled in theology and civil law, in the duties of magistrates and in the dialectics of religious controversy, entering the republic of Geneva, and conforming its ecclesiastical discipline to the principles of republican simplicity, established a party of which Englishmen became members and New England the asylum."[52]

The same radical and implacable differences which existed between the dissenters and the Episcopalians in England continued between them on this side of the Atlantic, and finally brought them into open conflict. The Episcopal Church, being the established Church of the English nation, having her supreme authority vested in the English sovereign, claimed the right to be the only Church to exist under the British flag. Hence the non-conformists could not find a place for the soles of their feet on which to rest wherever the Establishment had the power. Their only relief was in flight from the homes of their childhood and the graves of their fathers. They came to this land seeking, not wealth or fame, but a retreat in which to worship God and train up their children in the principles of their religion without incurring the wrath of princes or bringing upon them the terrors of inquisitors.

---

[52] *History of the United States*, vol. i, p. 266.

Not as the conqueror comes,
They, the true-hearted, came;
Not with the roll of the stirring drums,
And the trumpet that sings of fame.

Not as the flying come,
In silence and in fear; —
They shook the depths of the desert gloom
With their hymns of lofty cheer.

* * * *

There were men with hoary hair
Amidst the Pilgrim band;
Why had they come to wither there,
Away from their childhood's land?

There was woman's fearless eye,
Lit by her deep love's truth;
There was manhood's brow serenely high,
And the fiery heart of youth.

What sought they thus afar?
Bright jewels of the mine?
The wealth of seas? the spoils of war? —
They sought a faith's pure shrine.

Ay, call it holy ground,
The soil where first they trod!
They have left unstained what there they found—
Freedom to worship God.[53]

This they sought, and this they left to all succeeding ages,
but this they hardly found for themselves.

---

[53] Felicia Dorothy Hemans, *Landing of the Pilgrim Fathers.*

48

The land was too large and fair and fruitful to be given up to such independent and insubordinate religionists. The great Church of England must be planted and maintained wherever her sovereign swayed his royal sceptre. Therefore she speedily stretched herself across the seas, and took up her new abode in the Pilgrims' asylum, with all her authority and all her claims of divine rights of kings and apostolic succession. Wherever she could assert her power again in the new land the dissenters were made keenly to feel it. In Virginia and New York the people were taxed for her support, no matter what was their religious belief—taxed to maintain a hierarchy from which they had fled, and which they hated—taxed without representation in either Church or State. Even so late as 1707, Francis Makemie, a Presbyterian clergyman, was imprisoned by Lord Cornbury in New York City for being what the Anglicans called "a strolling preacher," and for spreading what they designated "pernicious doctrines." And up even "to the very moment of the Declaration of Independence the Presbyterians were denied a charter of incorporation" in New York. Thanks, everlasting thanks, to William Penn! All religionists were accorded, in his colony, equal rights with those who he called "the hot Church party."

Such, then, was the religious feature of the Revolutionary conflict; and it was one of the principal causes of the war for independence. That war was not by any means a mere civil and political strife. Religion was at the very heart's core of it. In 1815, John Adams wrote these significant words: "The apprehensions of Episcopacy contributed, fifty years ago, as much as any other cause to arouse the attention, not only of the inquiring mind, but of the common people, and urge them to close thinking on the constitutional power of Parliament over the colonies. . . Passive obedience and non-resistance in the most unqualified and unlimited sense were the

49

principles in government; and the power of the Church to decree rites and ceremonies, and the authority of the Church in controversies of faith, were explicitly avowed . . In Virginia the Church of England was established by law in *exclusion*, and *without toleration*, of any other denomination. In New York it displayed its essential character of intolerance. Large grants of land were made to it, while other denominations could obtain none; and even Dr. Rogers's congregation in New York, numerous and respected as it was, could never obtain a *legal title to a spot to bury its dead.*[54] In the same letter he adduces facts to prove what he terms "the bigotry, intrigue, intolerance and persecution" of the Establishment, and to confirm his statement that the threat of Episcopacy was one of the chief causes of the revolt of the colonies against Great Britain. It might be difficult to separate Monarchy and Episcopacy in the minds of the dissenting colonists, for they regarded them as twins; but to one who is acquainted with the struggles of the seventeenth and eighteenth centuries it will be evident enough that the dissenters feared Episcopacy quite as much as they feared monarchy, and that this fear was among the first and mightiest influences which lead to the war against King George.

In further confirmation of this we have most excellent and reliable testimony in the words of the Rev. Charles Inglis, rector of Trinity Church, New York, during the Revolution. He says, in a letter written to the Episcopal Church Missionary Society of London, Oct. 31, 1776: "The king's troops, totally abandoning this province, reduced the friends of government here to a most disagreeable and dangerous situation, especially the clergy, who were viewed with peculiar envy and malignity by the disaffected: for although *civil liberty was the ostensible* object, the bait flung out to catch the populace

---

[54] *Presbyterian Tracts*, vol. iv. p. 194.

at large and engage them in the rebellion, yet it is now past all doubt that an abolition of the Church of England was one of the principal springs of the dissenting leaders' conduct, and hence the unanimity of dissenters in this business. Their universal defection from government, emancipating themselves from the jurisdiction of Great Britain and becoming independent, was a necessary step to this grand object."[55] The Revolution, then, was, according to this testimony, more pre-eminently religious than political.

The dissenters had been driven to despair, and could endure the exactions of the Establishment no longer. The Episcopalians were unable to see how the Presbyterians could profess loyalty to the king while at the same time fomenting a spirit of independence. It seemed indeed a base hypocrisy; and it would have been so had it not been for the fact that it was *religious* as much as civil liberty for which they were contending. Hence the occasion of some of the first open outbreaks against the royal authority was the positive refusals of dissenters to pay the church-taxes levied upon them. This extract from one of the weekly papers of the time will serve to reveal the religious feelings engaged, along with the political, about six years before the Declaration of Independence: "This country will shortly become a great and flourishing empire, independent of Great Britain, enjoying its civil and religious liberty uncontaminated, and deserted of all control from bishops, the curse of curses, and from the subjection of all earthly kings. The corner-stones of this great structure are already laid, the materials are preparing, and before six years roll about the great, the noble, the stupendous fabric will be erected."[56] Whatever be the character of the spirit herein exhibited; certainly the prediction was most remarkably verified.

---

[55] *The Presbyterian*, December 1879.
[56] Jones's, *History of New York*, vol. 1, p. 24.

The king and the bishop stood side by side in the popular conception of the times; hence when war broke forth the dissenting churches were on the side of independence, and the Episcopal churches were as unanimously on the side of the Crown. This is not, however, so much to the discredit of the Episcopal clergy as it might now appear under the present order of things; for we are not to forget that they all, at that time, belonged to the Church of England, whose supreme authority on earth was vested in the reigning sovereign, to whom every clergyman of that Church had sworn allegiance.

The Reformation in England, it will be remembered, unlike that in other lands, proceeded from the sovereign, and not from the people. When Henry VIII, in a fit of passion, threw off the allegiance to the pope, he made himself chief pontiff of the Church. This relation was afterward maintained by the English sovereigns. Queen Elizabeth, in her moral sense base though in politics splendid, assured her prelates that had it not been for this great ecclesiastical authority in her possession, by which she could regulate and change the religion at her will, she never would have tolerated Protestantism.[57] Allow me here to quote from the Act of Uniformity, by which such ecclesiastical power was conferred upon the English monarch. She "may, by advice of her ecclesiastical commissioners, ordain and publish such ceremonies or rites as may be most for the advancement of God's glory and the edifying of the Church." Then, by another clause, Queen Elizabeth was allowed "to delegate her authority to any persons, being natural-born subjects, lay or clerical, who, as commissioners of and for the Crown, were empowered to visit, reform, redress, order, correct and amend all such errors, heresies, schisms, abuses, contempts and enormities whatsoever which, by any

---

[57] John Strype's *History of Bishop Matthew Parker*, vol. I, p. 217.

manner of spiritual or ecclesiastical power, authority or jurisdiction, can or may lawfully be reformed, ordered, redressed, corrected, restrained or amended."[58]

This, it will be observed, gives the Crown absolute control of the Church. As a High-Church historian has said, "Nothing can be more comprehensive than the terms of this clause."[59] "Whoever," says John Lingard, the eminent Roman Catholic historian, "will compare the powers given to this tribunal with those of the Inquisition which Philip II endeavored to establish in the Low Countries, will find that the chief difference between the two courts consisted in their names."[60]

Thus the liberties of the Church were suspended on the will of the reigning monarch, and her clergy were but the vicars for the Crown, which might, and sometimes did, suspend them from the exercise of their functions. Henry VIII by one stroke of his pen at one time suspended every prelate in England, and restored them only on their individual petition. And Elizabeth more than once threatened, with her usual vulgarity and profanity, to "unfrock" the clergy who manifested any opposition to her will.

It is not, therefore, surprising that the dissenting spirit of independence rebelled against such an Act of Uniformity, or that, their Church and living being at the mercy of the Crown, the clergy of the Establishment were unwilling to take up arms against the king. This was the very thing, however, to which the Calvinistic non-conformists would not submit. They believed, and maintained with their blood, that the sphere of the Church is distinct from that of the State, and that no king or Parliament has the right to bind the human conscience.

---

[58] *Presbyterian Tracts*, vol. iv, p. 19.
[59] Arthur Collier's *Ecclesiastical History*, vol. vi, p. 224.
[60] *History of England*, vol. v, p. 316.

Hence, in the war for American independence the dissenting churches arrayed themselves on the side of the colonies, and the Anglican Church arrayed itself on the side of the Crown. The independent and democratic spirit of Calvinism, cherished in the hearts of its adherents and nourished by their mixed assemblies and free discussions, rose up in rebellion against all despotic measures, whether of Church or State, and girded itself again for the great conflict on this Western continent. Montesquieu truly observes that "a religion which has no visible head is more agreeable to the independence of the climate than that which has one."[61] The Calvinists, recognizing no visibly supreme head in the Church, were sensitive to all interference by princes and men high in authority and in their restless spirit were quick to defend what they regarded as the inalienable rights of man. They felt, what Bancroft so justly declares, that "ecclesiastical tyranny is of all kinds the worst; its fruits are cowardice, idleness, ignorance and poverty."[62] And that they never would tolerate.

When the war broke out the Roman Catholic population of the colonies was not large. In 1759 it was about two thousand in Pennsylvania in a population of two hundred thousand, while the Germans, who were either Presbyterian or Lutheran in doctrine and church government, and who were brave defenders of civil liberty, numbered in the same colony about three-fifths of the entire population.

The Baptists, who are Calvinists, were not strong in the colonies. Their first church in this country was founded by Roger Williams, an eccentric, pious man. It was in 1639 that he came to the conclusion that immersion is the proper mode of baptism, and that he must be

---

[61] *The Spirit of the Laws*, vol. ii, p. 129
[62] *History of the United States*, vol. i, p. 289.

baptized again according to that method. But he could find no one who had been himself immersed to immerse him; hence he employed a layman, Ezekiel Holliman and about ten others. Thus was founded the first Baptist church in America. He himself, however, soon withdrew from the society, because he had come to the conclusion that his action in thus forming the Church had not been right or orderly. He was a most intense lover of civil and religious liberty, and contended most earnestly for all human freedom. Sixteen years before the Declaration of Independence the Baptists had fifty-six churches in the colonies. They have always been in the first ranks of the champions of civil liberty.

The Independents, or Congregationalists, were particularly strong in the Eastern colonies. At first they were Presbyterian in their church government, having elders and synods. They were, of course, Calvinists and rigid republicans, and their children, such as the Adamses and Franklin, were amongst the fathers of civil independency.

The Methodists had hardly a foothold in the colonies when the war began. In 1773 they claimed about one hundred and sixty members. Their ministers were almost all, if not all, from England, and were staunch supporters of the Crown against American independence. Hence, when the war broke out they were compelled to fly from the country. Their political views were naturally in accord with those of their great leader, John Wesley, who wielded all the power of his eloquence and influence against the independence of the colonies.[63] He did not foresee that independent American was to be the field on which his noble Church was to reap her largest harvests and that in that Declaration which he so earnestly opposed lay the security of the liberties of his followers.

---

[63] Bancroft, *History of the United States*, vol. vii, p. 261.

The Church of England—for there was then no American Episcopal Church—was specially strong in wealth and influence, particularly in Virginia and New York. As she was the Established Church, she held most of the civic and military offices.

Amongst the Calvinistic churches the Congregationalists and Dutch Reformed and Presbyterians were the leaders, and none of them took a more decided and active part in favor of independence than the Scotch-Irish Presbyterians. They threw into the movement all the fearlessness of the Scotch and all the fire and wit of the Irish character. Hence their speeches and sermons and papers and bulletins were at once irritating and amusing to their opponents. Bancroft accredits to them the glory of making the first bold move toward independence, and of lifting the first public voice in its favor.[64] To the Synod of the Presbyterian Church, convened in Philadelphia in 1775, belongs the responsibility—and may we not say the *glory?*—of being the first religious body to declare openly and publicly for a separation from England, and to counsel and encourage the people, who were then about taking up arms. It enjoined upon its people to leave nothing undone that could promote the end in view, and called upon them to pray for the Congress then assembled.[65]

Of course, a very large number of those who belonged to the Established Church engaged most heartily in the conflict in favor of independence, and freely gave their wealth and influence to secure it. One of the clergy, Jacob Duche, a native of Philadelphia and rector of Christ's Church, was for a time chaplain of the Continental Congress. He was an eloquent, liberal and charitable man, and for a while was truly and earnestly patriotic. Samuel Adams, the "Father of the Revolutionary War," a son of a

---

[64] *History of the United States*, vol. x, p. 77.
[65] *Scotch and Irish Seeds in American Soil*, p. 326.

deacon in the Old South Church, Boston, nominated Duche for the chaplaincy, saying that he (Adams) "was no bigot and could hear a prayer from a gentleman of piety and virtue who was at the same time a friend to his country." But as the conflict deepened, and the days grew darker, and many men's hearts were failing them, Duche lost confidence in the American cause, and wrote a letter to General Washington in which he pictured the hopelessness of resistance and urged him to cease his desperate and ruinous efforts. The general sent the letter to Congress, and Duche fled to England. Congress confiscated his property, and John Adams pronounced him to be "an apostate and traitor." In about ten years after Duche returned to Philadelphia, but never regained position or influence. The American people had accepted the estimate which Adams had put upon him.

It is to the glory of that Church also—and truly a glory it is—that the great general who led the Continental armies to victory, the "Father of our country," was a member of her household. It was through the strong and steady influence, against much opposition, of the two cousins, Samuel and John Adams, sons of pious deacons, and whose wives were daughters of dissenting clergymen, that Washington was appointed to the chief generalship.

And here let us note the happy influence of such women of the Revolution as the wives of the Adamses. This alone serves to reveal the spirit of Mrs. John Adams that the two things which first she taught her son, John Quincy, in those stirring and troublous times were the Lord's Prayer and Collin's Ode to the patriotic warriors of 1745:

> How sleep the brave who sink to rest
> By all their country's wishes blest!
> When Spring, with dewy fingers cold.
> Returns to deck their hallowed mould,
> She there shall dress a sweeter sod
> Than Fancy's feet have ever trod.

By fairy hands their knell is rung,
By forms unseen their dirge is sung,
There Honor comes, a pilgrim gray,
To watch the turf that wraps their clay,
And Freedom shall a while repair
To dwell, a weeping hermit, there.[66]

You can hear the freedom-loving spirit of that mother speaking through these lines as she impressed them upon the mind of their little son. Until the day of his death he could repeat them as easily as the Lord's Prayer. It was such women, behind the scenes, who were encouraging the hearts of the patriotic men and training the sons to take care of the cause of liberty.

It was these two great, independent sons of Independent deacons, John and Samuel Adams, who placed the command in the hands of him who was most worthy of it, and who, under the King of nations, led the colonies to such a splendid triumph. Perhaps it was glory enough for one Church that she could claim as her son George Washington, for the rector of Trinity Church, Charles Inglis, has left it on record that all her clergy in the New England colonies were on the side of the Crown. He says: "I have the pleasure to assure you that all the Society's missionaries, without excepting one, in New Jersey, New York, Connecticut, and, so far as I can learn, in the other New England colonies, have proved themselves faithful, loyal subjects in these trying times, and have, to the utmost of their power, opposed the spirit of disaffection and rebellion which as involved this continent in the greatest calamities. I must add that all the above clergy of our Church in the above colonies, though not in the Society's service, have observed the same line of conduct; and although their joint endeavors could not wholly

---

[66] William Collins (1721-1759), *How Sleep the Brave.*

pervert the rebellion, yet they checked it considerably for some time, and prevented many thousands from plunging into it who otherwise would certainly have done so."[67]

And in the same letter, to show the contrast, he says: "I do not know one of them (the Presbyterian clergy), nor have I been able, after strict inquiry, to hear of any, who did not, by preaching and every effort in their power, promote all the measures of Congress, however extravagant."

That, we say, they did; and on that their glory in the formation of this nation may well repose.

It has been made clear—first, that the fear of Episcopacy was one of the principal causes of the war for independence; and, second, that the Calvinists were, almost to a man, on the side of the colonies. It now remains for me to illustrate this second point, and show how the Calvinists, both from principle and moral necessity, struggled to procure the liberties under whose benign influence it is our privilege to live.

Montesquieu observes that there are two classes which talk of religion—the pious and the atheists. The one class speaks of what they love, and the other of what they fear.[68] Both have a right to be heard, for they are both in earnest. There is a great middle class of indifferents, who neither love nor fear religion enough to talk about it honestly and earnestly. These neither claim a hearing nor have a right to it. To them it is of slight importance whether they be Calvinists or Arminians. They are not interested enough in religion to inquire seriously as to where they stand. Neither cold nor hot, they are content to call the earnestness of the pious man "religious cant," and the honesty of the atheist a species of blasphemy.

---

[67] *Historical Notices of the Missions of the Church of England in the North American Colonies*, London, p. 328. Quoted by *The Presbyterian*, December 1879.
[68] *The Spirit of Laws*, vol. ii, p. 129.

As it is better to be either cold or hot than lukewarm, we are interested enough in religion, I hope, to know whereon we stand and the grounds on which we rest our hopes of eternal life. If we truly prize the blessings of civil and religious liberty, we cannot be uninterested in the agencies by which they were secured and the means by which they are maintained. Above all things, let us not belong to the army of religious indifferents.

The Calvinists, from their religious principles and by the free constitution of their churches, were naturally arrayed against monarchy when monarchy meant despotism. "The Scotch Kirk," says Lecky, "was by its constitution essentially republican . . . It was in this respect the very antipodes to the Anglican Church, both of which did all that lay in their power to consecrate despotism and strengthen [its] authority."[69] This holds good equally in regard to the American colonies and in regard to Great Britain and the nations of the European continent. The reason of it lies in the moral necessities of the case. Any one acquainted with the Roman Catholic Church will agree with De Tocquevllle when he says: "Catholicism is like an absolute monarchy."[70] It cannot, indeed, logically be anything else. Hence it results in that Roman Catholicism can never be looked upon merely as a religion. "It is," as a famous English writer observes,[71] "a great and highly organized kingdom, recognizing no geographical frontiers, governed by a foreign sovereign, pervading temporal politics with its manifold influence, and attracting to itself much of the enthusiasm which would otherwise flow in national channels. Its priests, in their intimate correspondence in many lands, the disciplined unity of their political action, the almost

---

[69] William E.H. Lecky, *History of England,* vol. ii, p. 46.
[70] *Democracy,* vol. I, p. 385.
[71] Lecky, *History of England,* vol. I, pp. 290, 291.

absolute authority they exercise over large classes, and their usually almost complete detachment from purely national and patriotic interests, have often in critical times proved a most serious political danger; and they have sometimes pursued a temporal policy eminently aggressive, sanguinary, unscrupulous and ambitious." This has been seen, more than once, in our own land, as it was in the denial of absolution by the Roman Catholic clergy of Canada to all who should befriend the cause of the colonies; while, on the other hand, the republican spirit of the Presbyterians in ecclesiastical affairs has always given shape to their political views, and inclined them to a stubborn resistance to all despotic powers. To this old Presbyterian, Calvinistic spirit was due the revolt of the American colonies. As Bancroft remarks, "Calvinism saw in goodness infinite joy, in evil infinite woe, and, recognizing no other abiding distinctions, opposed secretly, but surely, hereditary monarchy, aristocracy and bondage."[72]

Of private persons none, perhaps, had so much influence in arousing the American people to resistance as three young lawyers, Presbyterians, of New York City— William Smith, Jr., William Livingston and John Morin Scott. They were young men of family, education and fortune. The father of Smith (William, Sr.) was regarded as the leader and main support of the Presbyterian Church in the city. These three young men had been educated at Yale College, which was at the time a rigid Puritan institution, and "remarkable," as an Episcopal author observes, "For its republican principles . . . and its utter aversion to bishops and all earthly kings."[73] Being Presbyterians, and consequently flaming republicans, or Whigs, they banded themselves together for the expressed

---

[72] *History of the United States*, vol. ii, p. 462.
[73] Judge Jones, *History of New York*, vol. i, p. 5.

purpose of gaining the independence of the colonies. In prosecution of this end they formed, in concert with other kindred spirits, in 1752, the "Whig Club." In this club were such men of learning and wealth as Peter Van Brugh Livingston, David Van Horne, William Alexander, Robert R. Livingston, William Peartree Smith and Dr. John Jones. They met once a week, when republican speeches were made and republican songs were sung, and toasts were drunk to the heroes of Puritanism and republicanism, such as Oliver Cromwell, John Hampden and General Ludlow. By and by the club issued a political paper, called the *Independent Reflector,* and later another, entitled the *Watch-Tower.* By these and other means they aroused and nourished the spirit of independence, and encouraged and strengthened every effort made in pursuit of the desired object.

The members of the club were so generally Presbyterians that it was dubbed the "Presbyterian Junta"—a title given it in derision and scorn by the Episcopal loyalists. It was this body which did the reforming work in the metropolis. From it went forth the first effective call for a general Congress, though such a call had been spoken of before by Samuel Adams, a son of Deacon Adams of the Old South Church, Boston. Of this Samuel, who was married to the daughter of Rev. Samuel Checkley, pastor of the New South Church, Boston, it was said, "The foe of tyrants in every form, the friend of Virtue and her friends, the father of the American Revolution."

The members of this club, called also the "Sons of Liberty," sent forth a petition to Boston and Philadelphia, and through Philadelphia to every colony south, asking for a Congress composed of representatives from each of the colonies. This, says Bancroft, was the inception of the

Continental Congress.[74] And in this attitude of ceaseless agitation and bold defiance and restless struggling for independence did the members of this club stand through all the conflict, giving all that they held dear for the liberties of their land.

Another important factor in the independent movement was what is known as the "Mecklenburg Declaration," proclaimed by the Scotch-Irish Presbyterians of North Carolina, May 20, 1775, more than a year before the Declaration of Congress. It was the fresh, hearty greeting of the Scotch-Irish to their struggling brethren in the North, and their bold challenge to the power of England. They had been keenly watching the progress of the contest between the colonies and the Crown, and when they heard of the address presented by the Congress to the king, declaring the colonies in actual rebellion, they deemed it time for patriots to speak. Accordingly, they called a representative body together in Charlotte, NC, which by unanimous resolution declared the people free and independent, and that all laws and commissions from the king were henceforth null and void. In their Declaration were such resolutions as these: "We do hereby dissolve the political bands which have connected us with the mother-country, and hereby absolve ourselves from all allegiance to the British Crown." . . . "We hereby declare ourselves a free and independent people; are, and of right ought to be, a sovereign and self-governing association, under control of no power other than that of our God and the general government of Congress; to the maintenance of which we solemnly pledge to each other our mutual co-operation and our lives, our fortunes and our most sacred honor."

This was certainly a bold movement, and none, would have dared it but those who were ready to die. It was not

---

[74] *History of the United States*, vol. viii, p. 40.

done rashly. These men knew well what they were doing and what responsibilities they were assuming. None knew better. But, remembering their covenanting fathers, who had signed the old Covenant in Scotland with their blood, and believing that a just God does verily govern the affairs of the world, they laid their fortunes, lives and sacred honor on the altar of their country's freedom. That assembly was composed of twenty-seven staunch Calvinists, just one-third of whom were ruling elders in the Presbyterian Church, including the president and secretary; and one was a Presbyterian clergyman. The man who drew up that famous and important document was the secretary, Ephraim Brevard, a ruling elder of the Presbyterian Church and a graduate of Princeton College. Bancroft says of it that it was, "in effect, a declaration of independence as well as a complete system of govern- ment."[75] It was sent by a special messenger to the Con- gress in Philadelphia, and was published in the *Cape Fear Mercury,* and widely distributed throughout the land. Of course it was speedily transmitted to England, where it became the cause of intense excitement.

The identity of sentiment and the similarity of ex- pression in this Declaration and the great Declaration written by Jefferson could not escape the eye of the historian; hence Tucker, in his *Life of Jefferson,* says: "Every one must be persuaded that one of these papers must have been borrowed from the other." But it is certain that Brevard could not have "borrowed" from Jefferson, for he wrote more than a year before Jefferson; hence Jefferson, according to his biographer, must have "borrowed" from Brevard. But it was a happy plagiarism, for which the world will freely forgive him. In correcting his first draft of the Declaration it can be seen, in at least a few places, that Jefferson has erased the original words

---

[75] *History of the United States,* vol. viii, p. 40.

and inserted those which are first found in the Mecklenburg Declaration. No one can doubt that Jefferson had Brevard's resolutions before him when he was writing his immortal Declaration.

The spirit of the Mecklenburg resolutions was that of the Presbyterians throughout the entire conflict. They never wavered in their allegiance to the independent cause. They were always true to what Froude calls "the creed of republics in its first hard form"—the memorable reply of John Knox to Mary Stuart when she asked him, "If subjects, having the power, may resist their princes?" Knox replied, "If princes exceed their bounds, madam, they may be resisted even by power." They were, as Bancroft testifies, "the supporters of religious freedom in America. They were true to the spirit of the great English dissenter who hated all laws that were framed

> To stretch the conscience, and to bind
> The native freedom of the mind.

"It was," he continues, "from Witherspoon of New Jersey that Madison imbibed the lesson of perfect freedom in matters of conscience. When the constitution of New Jersey was formed by a convention composed chiefly of Presbyterians, they established perfect liberty of conscience without the blemish of a test."[76]

Out of that Presbyterian constitution has come the famous "Jersey justice," the extension of which over all the land would be an unspeakable blessing. The Rev. Dr. John Witherspoon, a native of Scotland and a lineal descendant of John Knox, was, in the Revolutionary time, president of Princeton College, and was the only clerical member of the Revolutionary Congress. He, as might be

---

[76] *History of the United States*, vol. ix, pp. 278, 279.

expected, earnestly and eloquently supported every measure adopted by Congress for securing independence. When the important moment came for signing the Declaration, and some of the members were hesitating to affix their names to it, he delivered an eloquent appeal, in which he said; "That noble instrument upon your table, which ensures immortality to its author, should be subscribed this very morning by every pen in the house. He that will not respond to its accents, and strain every nerve to carry into effect its provisions, is unworthy the name of a freeman. For my own part, of property I have some, of reputation more. That reputation is staked, that property is pledged, on the issue of this contest. And although these gray hairs[77] must soon descend into the sepulchre, I would infinitely rather they should descend thither by the hands of the public executioner than desert this crisis the sacred cause of my country."[78] All honor to him and to the Church and the principles which he so eloquently represented! That Church may well be proud of having her clergy so honorably represented among the signers of the Declaration of Independence.

Witherspoon remained in the Congress, excepting for a short period, till 1782, and contributed perhaps as largely as any one member to the patriotic cause. He was chairman of the committee to receive and consult with Baron Steuben, who had come to America to offer his services to the patriots, and he was the only one who could converse with the baron.[79] They conversed in French. The Congress was then sitting at York, Pennsylvania.

None of the colonies was more enthusiastic and self-sacrificing on behalf of independence than New Jersey, or *Nova Ceasarea,* the one represented by Witherspoon and

---

[77] He was then in the fifty-fourth year of his age.
[78] *Scotch and Irish Seed in American Soil,* p. 334.
[79] Spark's *Lives: "Steuben."*

the one so full of "Blue-stocking" Presbyterians. It was to
it that the patriots fled for refuge from New York on the
entrance of Howe's army into that city. It was amongst its
True Blues that the scattered and discouraged forces of
Washington found, again and again, recruits and
provisions and shelter and encouragement. A Tory
historian says that "not a stick of wood a spear of grass or
a kernel of corn could the British troops get in New Jersey
without fighting for it."[80] Her people had caught the spirit
of her eminent representatives in Congress and of her
republican college at Princeton, where so many of the
chief actors in the Revolution had been educated, and
hence they stood united and firm and enthusiastic through
all the conflict.

Another important man in the cause of independence
was the Rev. John Rodgers the leading Presbyterian
clergyman in New York City, and the first moderator of
the General Assembly of the Presbyterian Church in
America. He and John Mason, pastor of the Seceder
Church, and Livingston of the Dutch Church, and Laidley
of the English-Dutch Church, were among the patriotic
leaders in that city. Rodgers was born in Boston, of
parents who had emigrated from Londonderry, Ireland,
and his church in New York was large and wealthy and
influential. He had to fly from the city on the entrance of
the British troops, who seized his church and turned it into
a hospital. Congress acknowledged his patriotism and
ability by employing him on an important mission to the
South. He was chaplain of the State convention of New
York. He threw all his eloquence, influence and
possessions upon the side of the good cause, and did more
perhaps, in the beginning, to arouse the people than any
other clergyman.

[80] Jones, *History of New York*, vol. I, p. 171.

The following incident serves to reveal the political sentiment and movement of the clergy of New York City. It is given by an eye-witness and a prominent member of the Anglican Church. When Generals Washington, Charles Lee and Philip Schuyler were in their way to assume command of their respective armies, in 1775—Washington and Lee going to Boston, and Schuyler to Albany—they arrived in New York on a Sabbath morning in the month of June. And by whom were they met and welcomed to the city? By the volunteer companies, the members of the Provincial Congress of New York, the members of the City Committee and the pastors of the dissenting churches. Washington and Lee were members of the Episcopal Church, but there was not a clergyman of their Church to bid them welcome. These others, the Calvinists, met them, and conducted Washington to the house of a Calvinist, Mr. Leonard Lispenard, where he and his staff were bountifully entertained. But on that same day and in that same city another high officer arrived—General Tryon, the king's governor of the colony. And by whom was he met and welcomed? By all the king's officers and scores of his loyal subjects, prominent amongst whom were the clergy of the Episcopal Church. Nothing could more clearly mark the difference in political sentiment of these different clergymen and their churches. From that time Washington was about as much of a Presbyterian as an Episcopalian. When afterward he was commander in New York he made his headquarters with William Smith, a prominent Presbyterian. He himself attended, and ordered all his men to attend, the services of his chaplains, who were dissenting clergymen; and he elsewhere attended the dissenters' service and communed with them. He gave forty thousand dollars in bonds to establish a Presbyterian college in his native State, which took his name in honor of his munificent gift, becoming Washington College.

68

Thus I might trace through all that severe conflict the spirit of the Calvinists, and find it always the same—true to the cause of independence; indeed, the only unswerving champion of it. This is no more than prominent men, historians and clergymen on the other side have said. I could not employ language more definite and pointed than that of the Rev. Dr. Chandler, a clergyman of the Episcopal Church and a man of ability and note, when, in his plea for an American episcopate as distinct and different from the English, he said: "Republican principles cannot flourish in an Episcopal Church." Everywhere during all that conflict it was the Calvinists chiefly who were fighting for religious and civil liberty. Hence, when the bill of attainder was made out in New York against those who had been conspicuous in their efforts to defeat the colonies, there was not a dissenter's name found in it."[81]

But the influence of the free spirit of Calvinism in favor of the liberties of the colonies was not confined to the American continent; it was working heroically on the other side of the Atlantic. Two great Scotchmen, David Hume and Adam Smith, were everywhere proclaiming it in their own effective way, and compelling men to hear it. In the House of Commons also it was boldly and eloquently upheld by Erin's gifted son, Edmund Burke, as well as by Charles James Fox, of whom Dr. Johnson said, "Here is a man who has divided a kingdom with Caesar, so that it was a doubt which the nation should be ruled by, the sceptre of George III or the tongue of Mr. Fox." The memory of such champions of American liberty at the English court should be held for ever dear by the American people, for had it not been for such men, it is doubtful if the colonies could have succeeded. These great men felt that America's cause was the cause of liberty, and

---

[81] Jones, *History of New York, in loco.*

69

that, as Burke said, the establishment of the king's and the Church's power in America would become an apt, powerful and certain engine for the destruction of freedom in England.[82]

The Calvinistic philosophy had also taken a firm hold of the popular mind in Germany, where Kant, imbued with its liberty-loving spirit, was loosening the foundations of despotism and suffering persecution for his valiant defense of the American cause. France, too, was all aglow with the free, bounding, restless spirit of Calvinism—where Rousseau, in spite of the immorality of his life and the crudity of his theories, was conducting, through his political science, the same political warfare as that in America. His influence in advocating the rights of man contributed very largely to the forming of the alliance between France and the colonies, and to the unfurling of the royal standard alongside of the blue flag of the Covenanters, hoisted again in a new form over the American continent. It was Calvinistic France and Calvinistic America that were going forth in loving unity to fight on Western soil for the cause of human freedom. As our great historian observes, "Anti-prelatical Puritanism was embraced by anti-prelatical skepticism. The exile Calvin was welcomed home as he returned by the way of New England and the States where the Huguenots and Presbyterians prevailed . . . One great current of vigorous living opinion, which there was no power in France capable of resisting, swept through society, driving all the clouds in the sky in one direction. Ministers and the king and the nation were hurried along together."[83]

Thus Calvinism in Europe and Calvinism in America were leagued together for the promotion of the one great purpose. Their several currents, civil and spiritual, philosophical and religious, had run together, and were

---

[82] Buckle, vol. i, p. 345.
[83] Bancroft, *History of the United States,* vol. ix, pp. 501-503.

sweeping on in one great stream, bearing the colonies on to liberty. Out of Calvinistic Protestantism had arisen the great leaders who had issued their rousing calls to the nations for deliverance from mental and political bondage, and had combined their forces for securing the one great object. Rousseau had inflamed the youthful spirit of France with an intense desire for republican simplicity, and Edwards had summed up the political enthusiasm by declaring virtue to consist in universal love.

Thus, it was the Calvinists and their sons, at home and abroad, the Huguenots and Puritans and Independents and Presbyterians, who were banded and marshaled together in the eighteenth century for the laudable purpose of rescuing the liberties of men from the deadly grasp of a mediaeval political Arminianism.

Understanding, then, the history of the times referred to, we are not surprised to hear men say, as Leopold von Ranke, that "John Calvin was virtually the founder of America," or as Rufus Choate: "In the reign of Mary [of England] a thousand learned artisans fled from the stake at home to the happier states of continental Protestantism. Of these, great numbers—I know not how many—came to Geneva . . . I ascribe to that five years in Geneva an influence which has changed the history of the world. I seem to myself to trace to it, as an influence on the English character, a new theology, new politics, another tone of character, the opening of another era of time and liberty. I seem to myself to trace to it the great civil war in England, the republican constitution framed in the cabin of the Mayflower, the divinity of Jonathan Edwards, the battle of Bunker Hill, the independence of America."

Similar also is the testimony of Emilio Castelar, the eloquent Spanish statesman. He says: "The children of the Puritans founded the United States, a liberal and popular government, where human rights were placed above all ideas . . . They harmonized antagonisms which seemed eternal—stability with progress, order with liberty, pure democracy with obedience to the law, the widest freedom of different social tendencies with a powerful nationality and ardent patriotism, the humanitarian with the cosmopolite spirit, indomitable independence of the individual with religious respect to authority . . . The Anglo-Saxon democracy is the product of a severe theology learned by the few Christian fugitives in the gloomy cities of Holland and Switzerland, where the morose shade of Calvin still wanders . . . And it remains serenely in its grandeur, forming the most dignified, most moral, most enlightened and richest portion of the human race."[84]

So also Bancroft: "He that will not honor the memory and respect the influence of Calvin knows but little of the origin of American independence." . . . "The light of his genius shattered the mask of darkness which Superstition had held for centuries before the brow of Religion."

So also the Rev. Henry Ward Beecher: "It has ever been a mystery to the so-called liberals that the Calvinists, with what they have considered their harshly despotic and rigid views and doctrines, should always have been the staunchest and bravest defenders of freedom. The working for liberty of these severe principles in the minds of those that adopted them has been a puzzle. But the truth lies here: Calvinism has done what no other religion has ever been able to do. It presents the highest human ideal to the world, and sweeps the whole road to destruction with the most appalling battery that can be imagined."

"It intensifies, beyond all examples, the individuality of man, and shows in a clear and overpowering light his responsibility to God and his relations to eternity. It points out man as entering life under the weight of a tremendous responsibility, having, on his march toward the grave, this one sole solace—of securing heaven and escaping hell."

---

[84] *Harper's Magazine*, July, 1872.

"Thus the Calvinist sees man pressed, burdened, urged on, by the most mighty influencing forces. He is on the march for eternity, and is soon to stand crowned in heaven or to lie sweltering in hell, thus to continue for ever and ever. Who shall dare to fetter such a being? Get out of his way! Hinder him not, or do it at the peril of your own soul. Leave him *free* to find his way to God. Meddle not with him or with his rights. Let him work out his salvation as he can. No hand must be laid crushingly upon a creature who is on such a race as this—a race whose end is to be eternal glory or unutterable woe for ever and ever."[85]

I have thus traced for you, as briefly and accurately as the circumstances would permit, the workings of this great Calvinistic system of religion for the liberties of men; and it now only remains for me to remind you, and urge you to engrave it upon your heart, that on your *religion ever depends your freedom or your bondage.* It is a matter of supreme importance what doctrines you believe, what principles you adopt. On these you must erect the whole superstructure of your life for this world and for the world which is to come. By these arise or fall, live or die the governments of kingdoms and the privileges of citizens. If this grand republic shall ever become a despotism by any combination of centralized power, certain it is that it will not be by the spirit of Calvinism, or with the permission of the spiritual sons of those who gave it birth and cradled it in suffering and nourished it into maturity with their blood. With the history of the fathers before you, with a hell to be shunned and a heaven to be secured, you cannot be in doubt as to what principles you ought to adopt and what Lord and Master you ought to serve. Take these thoughtful lines of Wordsworth and weave them into the very framework of your being:

---

[85] *Plymouth Pulpit*, art. "Calvinism."

73

"Ungrateful Country, if thou e'er forget
The sons for who thy civil rights have bled!
How, like a Roman, Sidney bowed his head,
And Russel's milder blood the scaffold wet!
But these had fallen for profitless regret
Had not thy holy Church her champions bred,
And claims from other worlds inspirited
The star of Liberty to rise. Nor yet
(Grave this within thy heart!), if spiritual things
Be lost through apathy, or scorn, or fear,
Shalt thou thy humbler franchise support,
However hardly won or justly dear:
What came from heaven to heaven by nature clings,
And if dissevered thence, its course is short."

Calvinism
As a Moral Force

III

Calvinism

As a Moral Force

I come now to consider the very important question of the *moral influence* of Calvinism. Bearing in mind the law set forth in the Savior's saying, "By their fruits ye shall know them," we are to inquire as to the merits of Calvinism respecting the morals of its adherents.

In doing this we might rest the claims of Calvinism to a high standard of morality on a comparison between the morals of Roman Catholics—among whom Arminianism is carried out to its logical results[86]—and the morals of any denomination of Calvinists, the Huguenots, for example, or the Puritans, or Independents, or Presbyterians. Take any of these classes of Calvinistic believers, and it will be found that they are as eminent in virtue as the Romanists are conspicuous in vice. The Roman clergy are forward to attribute the prevailing crimes of modern society to the Protestant religion, but it needs only a glance at the facts

---

[86] Of course we do not mean to say that the Arminianism of the Romanist Church is responsible for the immoralities of that Church: we mean simply to contrast the morals of the most thorough Arminians with the morals of the most thorough Calvinists.

to dispel the illusion which they would have men believe. And while they are to charge upon the Protestants the sins to which they and their followers are most habitually addicted, they would, I believe, shrink from a strict comparison of the morals of any portion of their people with the morals of any portion of the Calvinists.

But Calvinism has had to meet not only the accusations of Roman Arminianism, but the allegations of many who claim for themselves the title of Protestant. There are to be found amongst Protestants those who look upon Calvinism as unfavorable to a sound morality, and who allege against it that it is a system of intellectual servitude, paralyzing to the moral and spiritual nature.

The eminent Dr. Channing employed all his ingenuity in "the moral argument" against Calvinism, and labored, not without some success, to make Calvinism odious and abhorrent. He says, in the height of his misinformed zeal, that it "outrages conscience and reason," and that it "owes its perpetuity to the influence of fear in palsying the moral nature." It might, perhaps, be difficult to account for such statements from one who was himself "the pupil of New England Christianity, the consummate flower of the old Puritanism, in his youth;" who was decided to a religious life through the influence of Jonathan Edwards and his Calvinistic uncle, the Rev. Henry Channing, and the great Calvinistic revival which swept over New England when he was as yet a young man; and who, as the Rev. Joseph Cook observes, "showed throughout life some touches from the fingers of the prophet of Geneva," and "whose glorious aspiration for moral greatness, which made him a reformer in things both secular and religious, was but the flowering out of some of the stern doctrines of Puritanism."[87] It abates materially, however, the force of Channing's statements to know that in the later and riper

---

[87] *Lectures: Miracles, Prophecy and Inspiration*, Prelude, March 8, 1880.

years of his life his religious system with which he endeavored to replace the Puritanism of his fathers has almost passed way as a living power, having been found "as inadequate to span the river of sin as a fishing-rod is to bridge the Mississippi."[88] If there is one characteristic of Calvinistic morality more prominent than another, it is its conscience. John Quincy Adams, a disciple of Channing, has called the Puritan colony of New England "a colony of conscience;" and Taine remarks that with the Calvinists "conscience only spoke."[89]

The two great springs by which men are moved are *sentiment* and *idea, feeling* and *conviction;* as these control, so the moral character will be shaped. The man of sentiment, of feeling, is the man of instability; the man of idea, of conviction, is the man of stability: he cannot be changed until his conscience first is changed. Now, the appeal of Arminianism is chiefly to the sentiments. Regarding man as having the absolutely free moral control of himself, and as able at any moment to determine his own eternal state, it naturally applies itself to the arousing of his emotions. Whatever can lawfully awaken the feelings it considers expedient. Accordingly, the senses, above all things, must be addressed and affected. Hence, the Arminian is, religiously, a man of feeling, of sentiment, and consequently disposed to all those things which interest the eye and please the ear. His morality, therefore, as depending chiefly upon the emotions, is, in the nature of the case, liable to frequent fluctuation, rising or falling with the wave of sensation upon which it rides. Calvinism, on the other hand, is a system which appeals to idea rather than sentiment, to conscience rather than emotion. In its view all things are under a great and perfect system of divine laws, which operate in defiance of

---

[88] Cook, *Independent*, March 18, 1880.
[89] Taine's *History of English Literature*, vol. i, p. 388.

feeling, and which must be obeyed at the peril of the soul. Regarding the sinner as unable of himself even to exercise faith unto salvation, it throws him not upon his feelings, but upon his convictions, and turns him away from man and all human efforts to the God who made him. "Its grand principle is the contemplation of the universe in God revealed in Christ. In all places, in all time, from eternity to eternity, Calvinism sees God."[90] Its thought is not *sentiment*, but *conviction*—not the arousing of the sensuous, but the quickening of the spiritual nature. Calvin considered it next to a crime to appeal to men's feelings simply in order to have them act. He desired rather to bring the rule of conscience into the practical life—to make the voice of God, speaking in the soul, the guide in all the conduct. He sought rather to *convince* men than to fill them with a transient sensation. Thus *a deep sense of duty* is the great thing in the moral life of the Calvinist. His first and last question is, *Is it right?* Of that he must first be convinced. Hence with him *conscience* has the first place in all practical questions.

You will observe how this idea of duty runs through all the Calvinistic philosophy, as in Reid's of Great Britain, Kant's of Germany, Jonathan Edwards' of America. In the Calvinistic conception God has marked out the way in which man is to walk—a way which he will not change; and man is required to walk in it, joyously or sorrowfully, with as much or as little sentiment as he pleases. Hence the Calvinist is not, religiously, a man of demonstrations, but rather a man of thoughtfulness; so that his morality, whatever it may be otherwise, is characterized by stability and strength, which may sometimes lapse into stubbornness and harshness. "He is troubled," says Taine, "not only about what he must believe, but about what he ought to do; he craves an

---

[90] Peter Bayne's, *Chief Actors in the Puritan Revolution*, p. 16.

80

answer to his doubts, but especially a rule for his conduct; he is tormented by the notion of his ignorance, but also by the horror of his vices; he seeks God, but duty also. In his eyes the two are but one."[91] "We have," he continues, "considered these Puritans as gloomy madmen, shallow brains and full of scruples. Let us quit our French and modern ideas, and enter into these souls: we shall find there something else than hypochondria—namely, a grand sentiment, 'Am I a just man? And if God, who is perfect justice, were to judge me at this moment, what sentence would he pass upon me?' Such is the original idea of the Puritans . . . The feeling of the difference there is between good and evil and had filled for them all time and space, and had become incarnate . . . They were struck by the idea of duty. They examined themselves by this light, without pity or shrinking; they conceived the sublime model of infallible and complete virtue; they were imbued therewith; they drowned in this absorbing thought all worldly prejudices and all inclinations of the senses . . . They entered into life with a fixed resolve to suffer and to do all, rather than deviate one step."[92]

Such was the morality of the men whom liberals (so called) and free-thinkers and free-lovers have endeavored to ridicule, and such the moral system which men claiming to be enlightened and truthful have said to be an "outrage upon conscience" and unfavorable to good morals. It is indeed the luster of its morality which has made it so conspicuous a mark for the shafts of the foe. The strictness of its purity arouses against it the passions of those who are conscious of being far below its just requirements. What is wanted today, and in all days in this world, is not less, but more, of the Calvinistic conscience, purity and rectitude.

---

[91] *History of English Literature*, vol. ii, p. 462.
[92] Ibid, p. 471.

Another prominent characteristic of Calvinistic morality is its *courageousness*. This follows from the former. Conscience and courage go together. Conscience makes "cowards" or heroes "of us all." To change the conscience you must first change the idea. But this is not easily done. Sentiment, or feeling, may pass through a thousand changes in a moment, and carry its possessor in so many directions; but conviction holds steadfastly on in the same unvarying way until by some brighter light it discovers its error and turns aside. Hence the men of conscience are, other things being equal, the brave men, the bold men, the courageous men. Calvinism, by appealing to conscience and emphasizing duty, begets a moral heroism which has been the theme of song and praise for three centuries. Channing's view was peculiarly distorted when he said that Calvinism "owes its perpetuity to the influence of fear in palsying the moral nature." Had he not read the history of the Reformation in Europe or of the Revolution in England? Had he so soon forgotten the moral heroism of the Puritans of his own New England? Fear, indeed, is one of the least potent elements in the Calvinistic system. Calvinism does teach a fear of God, a fear of sin and a fear of hell; and, if the Gospel be true, it becomes all men to have fear in that direction. That, surely, from which the Son of God died to redeem men ought to be feared as nothing else is. It is the loving forewarning of the Redeemer not to fear men, but to "fear Him who, after He hath killed, hath power to cast into hell. Yea, I say unto you, Fear him." Such a fear Calvinism does conscientiously and faithfully inculcate. Yet such is its tendency to deliver from a slavish bondage to fear that not a small class of men have looked upon it as a species of lofty fatalism, somewhat more divine than Islamism.

Certain it is that it gives no such place to fear as does the system of a rigid Arminianism. Consider the terrors brought to bear upon the mind by the Church of Rome and you get an idea of the fear-element of a strict Arminianism. Even of Arminianism as embodied in Methodism—so much more evangelical and moderate than that of Romanism—Lecky, who speaks with the cold, philosophic spirit of the rationalist, says: "A more appalling system of religious terrorism, one more fitted to unhinge a tottering intellect and to darken and embitter a sensitive nature, has seldom existed."[93] While I quote him not to justify him altogether in this judgment, I yet can well conceive of the terror to a sensitive soul of that dark uncertainty as to salvation, and of that ever-abiding consciousness of the awful possibility of falling away from grace after a long and painful Christian life, which is taught by Arminianism. To me such a doctrine has terrors which would cause me to shrink away from it for ever, and which would fill me with constant and unspeakable perplexities. To feel that I were crossing the troubled and dangerous sea of life dependent for my final security upon the actings of my own treacherous nature were enough to fill me with a perpetual alarm. If it is possible, I want to know that the vessel to which I commit my life is seaworthy, and that, having once embarked, I shall arrive in safety at my destination.

This is what the doctrines of Calvinism assure me. With its free grace, its effectual calling, its final perseverance and divine sovereignty, it affords me a consciousness of security in the midst of all my doubts, temptations and perplexities, it thus inspires its possessor with confidence, so that he can triumphantly say, "I am persuaded that he *shall keep* that which I have committed to him against that day." It thus dethrones fear, exalts confidence, and works in the mind the conviction that the interests committed to Christ are *kept* against all the possibility of loss, and that the man himself is immortal

---

[93] *History of England, Eighteenth Century*, vol. ii, p. 633.

until his work is done. Where such a conviction prevails, courage must follow. Hence the remark of the historian Bancroft: "A coward and a Puritan never went together."

For the courageous morality of the Calvinists one has only to look at the doings of the Inquisition in the Low Countries and at the martyrdoms of Cambray and the fires of Smithfield. Who were the martyrs but Calvinists? There is no other system of religion in the world which has such a glorious array of martyrs to the faith. Almost every man and woman who walked to the flames rather than deny the faith or leave a stain on conscience was the devout follower not only, and first of all, of the Son of God, but also of that minister of God who made Geneva the light of Europe. Is, then, the system one of paralyzing influence on the moral nature?

"I am going to ask you," says Froude, who is sometimes spoken of as an assailant of Calvinism, "to consider how it came to pass that if Calvinism is indeed the hard and unreasonable creed which modern enlightment declares it to be, it has possessed such singular attractions in past times for some of the greatest men that ever lived; and how, being, as we are told, fatal to morality, because it denies free-will, the first symptom of its operation wherever it established itself was to obliterate the distinction between sins and crimes, and to make the moral law the rule of life for states as well as persons. I shall ask you again, why, if it be a creed of intellectual servitude, it was able to inspire and sustain the bravest efforts ever made by man to break the yoke of unjust authority? When all else has failed; when patriotism has covered its face and human courage has broken down; when intellect has yielded, as Gibbon says with a smile or a sigh, "content to philosophize in the closet and abroad to worship with the vulgar; when emotion and sentiment and tender imaginative piety have become the handmaids of superstition, and have dreamt themselves into

84

forgetfulness that there is any difference between lies and truth,—the slavish form of the belief called Calvinism, in one or other of its many forms, has borne ever an inflexible front to illusion and mendacity, and has preferred rather to be ground to powder like flint than to bend before violence or melt under enervating tempt-ation." In illustration of this he mentions William the Silent, Luther, Knox, Andrew Melville, the regent Murray, Coligny, Cromwell, Milton, Bunyan, and says of them: "These were men possessed of all the qualities which give nobility and grandeur to human nature—men whose life was as upright as their intellect was commanding and their public aims untainted with selfishness; unalterably just where duty required them to be stern, but with the tenderness of a woman in their hearts; frank, true, cheerful, humorous, as unlike sour fanatics as it is possible to imagine any one, and able in some way to sound the keynote to which every brave and faithful heart in Europe instinctively vibrated."[94]

With this testimony every enlightened and impartial reader of history will agree. The men of commanding moral courage have been, and now are, those who have been most thoroughly and intelligently imbued with the Calvinistic doctrines. As another has said, "Calvin's fiery insistence of men and nations to God's moral law was, in the essence of it, noble, supremely noble, vibrating in true sympathy with the purest heroisms the world has ever seen." [95]

Another prominent characteristic of the Calvinistic morality is its *practicalness.* As we have seen it is a morality not of sentiment, but of idea; a morality which does not dissipate itself in the glow of a transient emotion, but which, seizing upon the conscience, works out in the

---

[94] *Calvinism*, pp. 7,8.
[95] Bayne, *Chief Actors in the Puritan Revolution*, p. 22.

practices and experiences of life; a morality not of a speculative nature, but of an earnest, active life struggling to make the conduct square with the requirements of the law of God. "What," says one, "is this Protestantism which is being founded in England? What is this ideal model which it presents? And which original conception is to furnish to this people its permanent and dominant poem? The harshest and most practical of all—that of the Puritans which, neglecting speculation, falls back upon action, binds human life in a rigid discipline, imposes on the soul continuous effort, prescribes to society a cloistral austerity, forbids pleasure, commands action, exacts sacrifices, and forms the moralist, the laborer, the citizen. Thus is it implanted, the great English idea—I mean that man is before all a free and moral personage, and that, having conceived alone in his conscience and before God the rule of his conduct, he must employ himself completely in applying it within himself, beyond himself, obstinately, inflexibly, by a perpetual resistance opposed to others and a perpetual restraint imposed upon himself."[96]

This brilliant writer calls it the "harshest" of all religious conceptions. To this we would by no means assent, unless harshness means obedience to God's laws and resistance to sin. That may indeed be considered harsh. The child may deem it hard treatment to be compelled to be truthful; the criminal may consider it a cruelty to be punished for his crimes; and he who wishes to live in the violation of moral principles may regard it as an outrage upon his liberty to be reminded of his guiltiness and warned of its penalty. In this sense the Calvinistic morality is "harsh," exceeding harsh—harsh, indeed, as Nature's laws—but it lays upon man not one exaction which it does not find already laid upon him by the God who made him.

---

[96] Taine, *English Literature*, vol. ii, pp. 316, 317.

It is this *practicalness* of the Calvinistic morality which has ever made it so beneficent. It is this which has formed its adherents into the most moral of all classes of human society—which gave to the Puritans the very title which is significant of their eminent moral qualities, and transformed the idle and slothful into the industrious and respected citizen. "Grave as we may count the faults of Calvinism," says one who is not at all given to lavish compliments upon it, "alien as its temper may in many ways be from the temper of the modern world, it is in Calvinism that the modern world strikes its roots; for it was Calvinism that first revealed the worth and dignity of man. Called of God and heir of heaven, the trader at his counter and the digger in his field suddenly rose into equality with the noble and the king."[97] The same author also accredits to Calvinism the formation of that sacred institution, the English Home, saying "Home, as we conceive it, was the creation of the Puritans." When there was no such institution in the world as Home; when the family existed without the sacred ministries of domestic life; when the woman was but the slave or the idol or the amusement of the man, as his temper or power or will might dictate; when the worst of vices were practiced within the domestic circle,—the Calvinists, by their constant aim at self-control, and their perpetual endeavor for the purity of morals, and their high regard for the marriage-covenant as symbolical of their relations to Christ, and their belief in the sublime possibilities of the woman as the man, formed, out of a loose and corrupt society, the hallowed shrine where the holiest affections are brought into play, and around which the fondest recollections of man cluster. That they did this one thing— formed the Christian Home—entitles them to the imperishable gratitude of mankind.

---

[97] John R. Green, *A Short History of the English People*, vol. ii, p. 280.

Let this also be remembered as a diadem upon the brow of Calvinistic morality: that in all the history of the Puritans there *is not an example of a divorce.* That is enough to offset the modern liberalistic cry against Puritanical strictness. Is it not Puritanism which modern society needs to purify and sweeten its corrupt and bitter waters and to give a healthful tone to all its moral life? "The Calvinists were the men," says Froude, "who abhorred, as no body of men ever more abhorred, all conscious mendacity, all impurity, all moral wrong of every kind so far as they could recognize it. Whatever exists at this moment in England and Scotland of conscientious fear of doing evil is the remnant of the convictions which were branded by the Calvinists into the people's hearts."[98] They were they "who attracted to their ranks almost every man in Western Europe that hated a lie."

"There is no system," says Henry Ward Beecher, "which equals Calvinism in intensifying, to the last degree, ideas of moral excellence and purity of character. There never was a system since the world stood which puts upon man such motives to holiness, or which builds batteries which sweep the whole ground of sin with such horrible artillery."[99] "Men may talk as much as they please against the Calvinists and Puritans and Presbyterians, but you will find that when they want to make an investment they have no objection to Calvinism or Puritanism or Presbyterianism. They know that where these systems prevail, where the doctrine of men's obligation to God and man is taught and practiced, there their capital may be safely invested."[100] "They tell us," he continues, "that Calvinism plies men with hammer and with chisel. It does;

---

[98] *Calvinism*, p. 44.
[99] *Leading Thoughts of Living Thinkers.*
[100] *Even. Sermon*, Feb. 10, 1860.

and the result is monumental marble. Other systems leave men soft and dirty; Calvinism makes them of white marble, to endure for ever."

You may examine all the history of Christian people and of religious systems and you will not find any more eminent for piety and morality than the Calvinists. In charity, in liberality, in industry, in temperance, in purity of life, they stand without a superior—perhaps without an equal. Compare the Huguenots and Jansenists, who were Calvinists, with their countrymen, the Romanists and Jesuits, who were Arminians. Were not the former as illustrious in virtue as the latter were notorious for immorality? "The destruction of the former by the Revocation of the Edict of Nantes was," says Lecky, "the destruction of the most solid, the most modest, the most virtuous, the most generally enlightened element in the French nation, and it prepared the way for the inevitable degradation of the national character, and the last serious bulwark was removed that might have broken the force of that torrent of skepticism and vice which, a century later, laid prostate, in merited ruin, both the altar and the throne."[101]

The morality of the Huguenots, whether suffering persecution at home or enduring the trials of exile abroad, was the wonder of both friend and foe. Looking back, says one, at the sufferings of those of them who remained in France after the Revocation of the Edict, and at the purity, self-denial, honesty and industry of their lives, and at the devotion with which they adhered to religious duty and the worship of God, we cannot fail to regard them as amongst the truest, greatest and worthiest heroes of their age. "When society in France was falling to pieces; when its men and women were ceasing to believe in themselves and in each other; when the religion of the state had become a

---

[101] *English History, Eighteenth Century*, vol. I, pp. 264, 265.

mass of abuse, consistent only in its cruelty; when the debauchery of its kings had descended through the aristocracy to the people, until the whole mass was becoming thoroughly corrupt,"—Huguenots were the only pure and true men—the only men who were moved by great ideas or controlled by honest convictions—the only men who were willing to die rather than forsake the worship of God according to the Scriptures and conscience.[102]

Outside of the circle of the Huguenots there was indeed but little that deserved the name of morality in France. Their honesty was so remarkable that even among their bitterest enemies it was proverbial. To be "honest as a Huguenot" was deemed the highest degree of integrity. And while they were stigmatized by the Roman Catholics as "heretics," "atheists," "blasphemers," "monsters vomited forth of hell," and the like, not one accusation was brought against the morality and integrity of their character. "The silence of their enemies on this head is," says Smiles, "perhaps the most eloquent testimony in their favor." "They were," says the same author, "what the Puritan was in England and the Covenanter in Scotland; and that the system of Calvin should have developed precisely the same kind of men in these three several countries affords a remarkable illustration of the power of religious training in the formation of character."[103]

Now, what could have made the difference in moral character between these French Calvinists and Arminians but their different religions? They were of one nation and one tongue, and frequently of one household, having the same natural qualities and affections; but they had a different creed, and that tells the tale.

---

[102] Samuel Smiles, *Huguenots in France*, p. 275.
[103] Ibid., p. 134.

Look, too, at Scotland before and after Knox and his co-laborers effected the Scottish Reformation. Arminianism, as exemplified in the Church of Rome, had the training of that people for centuries; and what had it made of them? Something less than human. Gross darkness covered the land and brooded like an eternal nightmare upon all the faculties of the people. Poverty, squalor, ignorance, vice and wretchedness were the prevailing characteristics of society. But see the quick and marvelous change effected when once the free doctrines learned by Knox at Geneva flashed in upon their minds. It was as the sun rising in his fullness at midnight. And in their later history, so long as they remained untainted with other beliefs, their morality was the wonder of the world. The celebrated Dr. Chalmers says: "It may be suspected that although a theology is the minister of peace, it cannot be the minister of holiness. Now, to those who have this suspicion, and who would represent the doctrine of justification by faith—that article, as Luther calls it, of a standing or falling Church—as adverse to the interests of virtue, I would put one question and ask them to resolve it. How comes it that Scotland, which, of all the countries of Europe, is the most signalized by the rigid Calvinism of her pulpits, should also be the most signalized by the moral glory that sits on the aspect of her general population? How, in the name of mystery, should it happen that such a theology as ours is conjoined with perhaps the yet most uninitiated peasantry among the nations of Christendom? The allegation against our churches is that in the argumentation of our abstract and speculative controversies the people are so little schooled to the performance of good works. And how, then, is it that in our courts of justice, when compared with the calendars of our sister-kingdom, there should be so vastly less to do with their evil works? It is certainly a most important experience, that in that country where there is

91

the most of Calvinism there should be the least of crime; that what may be called the most doctrinal nation of Europe should, at the same time, be the least depraved; and that the land wherein people are most deeply imbued with the principles of salvation by grace should be the least distempered either by their week-day profligacies or their Sabbath profanations."[104]

That is certainly a remarkable coincidence that where there is the most of Calvinism there is the least of crime, if Calvinism be unfavorable to morality. Similar also are the results wherever the doctrines of Calvinism are honestly and intelligently embraced. There the people practice such a rigid code of morality as subjects them to the sneering remarks of those who adopt a lower standard and entertain but few conscientious scruples regarding their conduct. The bigotry, narrowness and intolerance of which the Calvinists have been so often accused will generally prove to be the virtues which adorn human society and make civilization a possibility. Their "bigotry" is chiefly devotion to righteousness; their "narrowness," their fear of swerving from the "narrow way" which leadeth unto life; their "intolerance," the impatience of their zeal for the establishment of their Redeemer's kingdom upon earth. Such men will indeed appear, at times intolerant, through the intensity of their enthusiasm and their impatience with the sophistries by which many endeavor to conceal or excuse their follies and vices; but it is the intolerance of the good housewife, who brushes away the moths and cobwebs and makes the dwelling habitable; it is the intolerance of the fresh breeze, which sweeps away the poisonous vapors and gives to the atmosphere the elements of life.

"The Calvinists," says Froude, "have been called intolerant; but intolerance of an enemy who is trying to

---

[104] Sermon: *The Respect Due to Authority.*

kill you seems to me a pardonable state of mind. It is no easy matter to tolerate lies, clearly convicted of being lies, under any circumstances; specially, it is not easy to tolerate lies which strut about in the name of religion."[105] Of such things the gospel of Christ is eternally intolerant.

I cannot close this chapter without adverting, for a moment, to the moral character and worth of the Calvinists of New England—men whose strict and rigid morality has become a proverb. They have been spoken of and pointed at scornfully, as if they were only fanatics. And yet, amongst all the people in the American colonies, they stood morally without peers. They were the men and women of *conscience,* of *sterling convictions.* They were not, indeed, greatly given to sentimentalism. With mere spectacular observances in religion they had no sympathy. Life to them was an experience too noble and earnest and solemn to be frittered away in pious ejaculations and emotional rhapsodies. They believed with all their soul in a just God, a heaven and a hell. They felt, in the innermost core of their hearts, that life was short and its responsibilities great. Hence their religion was their life. All their thoughts and relations were imbued with it. Not only men, but beasts also, were made to feel its favorable influence. Cruelty to animals was a civil offence. In this respect they were two centuries in advance of the bulk of mankind. They were industrious, frugal and enterprising, and consequently affluence followed in their path and ascended to their children and children's children. Drunkenness, profanity and beggary were things little known to them. They needed neither lock nor burglar-proof to secure their honestly-gotten possessions. The simple wooden bolt was enough to protect them and their wealth where honesty was a rule of life. As the result of such a life they were healthy and vigorous. They lived

---

[105] *Calvinism,* p. 43.

long and happily, reared large and devoted families, and descended to the grave "like as a shock of corn cometh in his season," in peace with God and their fellow-men, rejoicing in the hope of a blessed resurrection.

It is said that they believed in "witches." Well, what if they did? That was the belief of their age. Men who have been a glory to the world believed in witches. But the Puritans abandoned the belief with penitence long before it was given up by others whose names are honored household words. Long after them—so late as the latter half of the last century—John Wesley, whose life has been an ornament to the world, advocated belief in witchcraft with all his accustomed ability and zeal. He declared with the utmost emphasis his belief in it, and attributed its downfall to skepticism. He believed that in giving it up a man was in effect giving up the Bible. He said: "I cannot give up to all the deists in Great Britain my belief in the existence of witchcraft till I give up the credit of all history, sacred and profane."[106]

We do not believe that now. But so the great and good Wesley believed. Let not, therefore, such a belief be attributed solely to the Puritans of New England, for they abandoned it long before it ceased to exist in Old England. They, indeed, were, as Bancroft observes, "of all contemporary sects the most free from credulity," . . . and "their transient persecutions in America were in self-defense, and were no more than a train of mists hovering of an autumn morning over the channel of a fine river that diffused freshness and fertility wherever it wound."[107]

Thus we might continue to trace the moral influence of this great system of religious belief, and should find that no other system in the world has produced such an array of moral heroes. Its illustrious names everywhere

---

[106] Lecky, *History of England, Eighteenth Century,* vol. ii., p. 645.
[107] *History of the United States,* vol. I, pp. 463, 464.

crowd the pages of history, and by its fruits it is known the world over.

And has its glory departed with the fathers, and left but the *name* with the children? It cannot be, if God be true and the world and life be not a delusion. Its truths are eternal as the laws of God, and its motives are as mighty today as of old. There is the same omniscient God to judge us, and the same hell to be shunned and the same heaven to be secured. Human nature is still the same depraved thing; and the same blood of the Lamb and fire of the Spirit are requisite unto life. Our time here is but the same short day; the fashion of the world still passeth away; and into the solemn realities of eternity we too must speedily enter. Ah, yes; but have we gotten hold of the truths of God and the responsibilities of life as the fathers had? Has the Spirit of God burned the real meaning of life into our souls as into theirs? In the grand privileges which we possess, sitting under our peaceful vines and fig trees, fearing no storm and knowing no alarm, may we not let life slip away, to be aroused at last to the awful realization of its eternal loss? Oh, that we might know the time—that this is the day of salvation!

Calvinism
As an Evangelizing Force

IV

Calvinism
As an Evangelizing Force

IN this chapter our inquiry will be as to the *evangelizing* force of Calvinism. Has Calvinism, as compared with other systems of religious doctrine, shown itself to have been a power in the evangelization of the world? This is the most important question connected with any system of belief. All other questions are, in every Christian's opinion, subordinate to this. To save sinners and convert the world to a practical godliness must be the chief, the first and last, aim of every system of religion. If it does not respond to this, it must be set aside, however popular it may be.

The question, then, before us is, not whether the system of doctrines called Calvinism is the most acceptable and popular with the world, but whether it is eminently adapted to the conversion of sinners and the edification of believers.

In determining this I shall proceed, as in the preceding chapters, according to the law, "The tree is known by its fruit."

We may, however, premise, on the ground of the doctrines included in this system, that it is certainly most favorable to the spread of Christianity. Its doctrines are all taken directly from the Scriptures. The word of God is its only infallible rule of faith and practice. Even its doctrine of predestination, or election, which most men dislike, but which all Christians practically believe and teach, is granted by some of its bitterest opponents to be a transcript of the teachings of the New Testament.

The historian Froude says: "If Arminianism most commends itself to our feelings, Calvinism is nearer to the facts, however harsh and forbidding those facts may seem."[108] And Archbishop Whately says the objections against it "are objections against the facts of the case." So Spinoza and John Stuart Mill and Buckle, and all the materialistic and metaphysical philosophers, "can find," says an eminent authority, "no better account of the situation of man than in the illustrations of St. Paul; 'Hath not the potter power over the clay, to make one vessel to honor and another to dishonor?'" There never has been, and it is doubtful if there ever can be, an Arminian philosophy. The facts of life are against it; and no man would attempt to found a philosophy on feeling against fact.

Arminian theologians thought they had discovered the starting-point for a systematic philosophy and theology in the doctrine of "free-will;" but even that was swept away from them by the logic of Jonathan Edwards, and it has continued to be swept farther and farther away by Buckle and Mill and all the great philosophers. Hence it comes that to this day there is not a logical and systematic body of Arminian divinity. It has as in the Methodist Church, a brief and informal creed in some twenty-five articles, but it has neither a Confession of Faith nor a complete and logical system of doctrine.[109] To make such a system it

---

[108] *Calvinism,* p. 6.
[109] E.P. Humphrey's *Our Theology in its Developments,* p. 68, etc.

must overthrow the philosophy of the world and the facts of human experience; and it is not likely to do that very soon.

Now, the thought is, must not a theology which agrees with the facts of the case, which recognizes the actual condition of man and his relations to God, be more favorable to man's salvation than one which ignores the facts?

This is confirmed by the nature of the particular doctrines involved. We freely agree with Froude and Macaulay that Arminianism, in one aspect of it, is "more agreeable to the feelings" and "more popular" with the natural heart, as that which exalts man in his own sight is always more agreeable to him than that which abases him. Arminianism, in denying the imputation of Christ's righteousness to the believer, in setting him on his own works of righteousness, and in promising him such perfection in this life as that there is no more sin left in him—or, in the words of John Wesley, a "free, full and present salvation from all the guilt, all the power and *all the* in-being of sin"[110]—lays the foundation for the notions of works of supererogation, and that the believer, while in a state of grace, cannot commit sin. It thus powerfully ministers to human pride and self-glorification. Calvinism, on the other hand, by imputing Christ's righteousness to the believer, and making the sinner utterly and absolutely dependent on Christ for his salvation, cuts away all occasion for boasting and lays him low at the foot of the cross. Hence it cannot be so agreeable to the feelings of our carnal heart. But may it not be more salutary, nevertheless? It is not always the agreeable medicine which is the most healing. The experience of the apostle John is one of frequent occurrence, that the little book which is sweet as honey in the mouth is bitter in the belly. Christ

---

[110] James P. *Gladstone's Life of Whitefield*, p. 199.

crucified was a stumbling-block to one class of people and foolishness to another, and yet he was, and is, the power of God and the wisdom of God unto salvation to all who believe.

The central doctrine of Calvinism, as an evangelistic power, is that which Luther called "the article of a standing or a falling Church"—"justification by faith alone, in the righteousness of Christ alone." And is not that the doctrine of the gospel? Where does the Holy Spirit ascribe the merit of any part of salvation to the sinner?

But aside from that question, which it is not my purpose here to argue, would not reason dictate that that doctrine is most conducive to salvation which makes most of sin and most of grace?

Rowland Hill once said that "the devil makes little of sin, that he may retain the sinner." It is evident at once that the man who considers himself in greatest danger will make the greatest efforts to escape. If I feel that I am only slightly indisposed, I shall not experience much anxiety, but if I am conscious that my disease is dangerous, I will lose no time in having it attended to. So if I feel, according to Arminianism, that my salvation is a matter which I can settle myself at any moment, even in the last gasp of dissolution, I shall be prone to take my time and ease in deciding it; but if, according to Calvinism, I feel that I am dependent upon God for it, whose pleasure, and not my own, I am to consult, I will naturally give more earnest heed to it.

Thus reason brings forward her vindication of Calvinism against the allegation that it is not favorable to the pursuit of salvation.

But perhaps some one may reply, "Has not the Methodist Church been more successful in her efforts to evangelize the world than any Calvinistic Church?" In answer I would say that I will give way to no one in my high estimate of that Church's piety and zeal and progress.

I thank God, with all my heart, for what she has done, and I pray that she may never flag in her energy and success in winning souls to Jesus Christ. I admire her profoundly, and her noble army of men and women enlisted in the Master's service. May she ever go on, conquering and to conquer, until we all meet as one on the great day of the triumph of the Lamb!

But bear in mind that the aggressive Church has no well-defined system of doctrine, and that her Arminianism is of a very mild type, coming nowhere near that of High-Churchism or Roman Catholicism. Wherein lay the elements of her power and progress? I do not believe, and I am confident it cannot be shown, that they lie in her Arminianism or in the doctrines common to all the Christian churches, such as sin, justification, regeneration and holiness, and in her admirable system of itinerancy, by which she keeps all her stations manned and sends forward fresh men to every new field. Let her preach Arminianism strictly and logically, and she will soon lose her aggressiveness, or become another institution than an evangelical Church of Christ.

Furthermore, Arminianism in the Methodist Church is but a century old. It has never passed through the years or the confusions through which Calvinism has passed. Will it continue in the ages to come to be the diffusive power which it has been for these years past? Of this I am persuaded, looking at the history and workings of religious opinions in the past: that the Church will be constrained in time to put forth a systematic and logical Confession of Faith,[111] out of which she will either drop all peculiarly Arminian doctrines, and so secure her permanency, or in which she will proclaim them, and by that means will inject the poison of death, as an *evangelizing* body, into

---

[111] I do not forget, and do not disparage, Richard Watson's *Theological Institutes.*

her system. A thorough Arminianism and a practical evangelism have never yet remained long in loving harmony. Look at the history of doctrines as illustrated in the history of the Church of Rome, and you will see this clearly attested. Arminianism, in its principles, had been in operation in that Church for centuries when the Reformation broke forth, and what evangelistic work had it done? It had indeed converted almost the entire world, but to what had it converted it? It had formed and established the largest and most powerful Church which the world has ever seen, but what had it done for the salvation of human bodies and souls? It had made Romanists, but it had not made Christians equally as numerous. Was it not the very principles of the Calvinistic theology which flashed light upon the thick darkness, and threw fire into the corrupt mass, and lifted up the banner of the cross, so long trodden under a debased hierarchy, and revived the ancient faith of the Church, and established the great Protestant and evangelical denominations of Christians? Who but Calvinists—or, as formerly called, Augustinians—were the forerunners of the Reformers? Such was Wycliffe, "the morning star of the Reformation;" such was John of Goch and John of Wesalia and John of Wessel, "the light of the world;" and Savonorola of Florence, who thundered with such terrible vehemence against the sins of the clergy and people, who refused a cardinal's hat for his silence, saying, "he wished no red hat, but one reddened with his own blood, the hat given to the saints"—who even demanded the removal of the pope, and, scorning all presents and promises and honors on condition of "holding his tongue," gave his life for the holy cause—another victim of priestly profligacy and bloodthirstiness. Every great luminary who in the Church immediately preceded the greater lights of the Reformation was in principle a Calvinist. Such also were the great national Reformers, as Luther of Germany,

Zwingle of Switzerland, Calvin of France, Cranmer of England, Knox of Scotland. "Although each movement was self-originated, and different from the others in many permanent characteristics,"[112] it was thoroughly Calvinistic. These men were driven to this theological belief, not by their peculiar intellectual endowments, but from their study of the word of God and the moral necessities of the Church and the world. They felt that half measures were useless—that it was worse than folly to seek to unite a system of saving works with a system of saving faith. So "Calvinism in its sharp and logical structure, in its moral earnestness, in its demand for the reformation of ecclesiastical abuses, found a response in the consciences of good men."[113] It was it which swept, like a prairie-fire, over the Continent, devouring the fabric of works of righteousness. He who is most familiar with the history of those times will most readily agree with the startling statement of Dr. Cunningham (successor to Dr. Chalmers), that, "next to Paul, John Calvin has done most for the world."

So thoroughly was the Reformed world Calvinistic three hundred years ago that it was almost entirely Presbyterian.[114] The French Protestant Church was as rigidly Presbyterian as the Scotch Church. "There are many acts of her synod," says the late Dr. Charles Hodge, "which would make modern ears tingle, and which prove that American Presbyterianism, in its strictest forms, is a sucking dove compared to that of the immediate descendants of the Reformers."[115]

There was, of course, as there always has been, greater diversity in the matters of church government than

---

[112] Dr. Hodge.
[113] Dr. Fisher, *History of the Reformation*
[114] Dr. Breed's *Presbyterianism Three Hundred Years Ago.*
[115] *Const. Hist.*

in the doctrines of faith; yet even in these there was an almost unanimous agreement that the presbyterial was the form of government most in accord with the teachings of Scripture. Dr. John Reynolds, who was in his day regarded as perhaps the most learned man in the Church of England, said, in answer to Brancroft, chaplain to the archbishop, who had broached what was then called "the novelty" that the bishops are a distinct order superior to the ordinary clergymen, "All who have for the past five hundred years endeavored the reformation of the Church have taught that all pastors, whether they be called bishops or priests, are invested with equal authority and power; as, first, the Waldenses, next Marsilius Patavianus, then Wycliffe and his scholars, afterward Huss and the Hussites, and, last of all, Luther, Calvin, Brentius, Bullinger and Musculus. Among ourselves we have bishops, the queen's professors of divinity in our universities and other learned men consenting therein, as Bradford, Lambert, Jewel, Pilkington, etc. But why do I speak of particular persons? It is the common Judgment of the Reformed churches of Helvetia, Savoy, France, Scotland, Germany, Hungary, Poland, the Low Countries and our own."[116]

If we now turn to the fruits of Calvinism in the form of devoted Christians and in the number of churches established, we shall see that it has been the most powerful evangelistic system of religious belief in the world. Consider with what amazing rapidity it spread over Europe, converting thousands upon thousands to a living Christianity. In about twenty-five years from the time when Calvin began his work there were two *thousand* places of Calvinistic worship, with almost *half a million of worshippers,* in France alone. When Ambrose Willie, a man who had studied theology at the feet of Calvin in Geneva, preached at Ernonville Bridge, near Tournay, in

---

[116] *Presbyterianism Three Hundred Years Ago,* pp. 24, 25.

1556, twenty thousand people assembled to hear him. Peter Gabriel had also for an audience in the same year, near Haarlem, "tens of thousands;" and we can judge of the theological character of this sermon from his text, which was, "For by grace are ye saved through faith; and that not of yourself; it is the gift of God: not of works, lest any man should boast; for we are his workmanship, created in Christ Jesus unto good works, which God hath before ordained that we should walk in them."[117]

These are but two of the many examples of the intense awakening produced by the earnest preaching of the Calvinistic doctrines. So great were the effects that in three years after this time a General Synod was held in Paris, at which a Confession of Faith was adopted. Two years after the meeting of the Synod—that is in 1561—the Calvinists numbered *one-fourth* of the entire French population.[118] And in less than half a century this so-called harsh system of belief had penetrated every part of the land, and had gained to its standards almost one-half of the population and almost every great mind in the nation. So numerous and powerful had its adherents become that for a time it appeared as if the entire nation would be swept over to their views. Smiles, in his *Huguenots in France*,[119] says: "It is curious to speculate on the influence which the religion of Calvin, himself a Frenchman, might have exercised on the history of France, as well as on the individual character of the Frenchman, had the balance of forces carried the nation bodily over to Protestantism, as was very nearly the case, toward the end of the sixteenth century." Certain it is that the nation would have had a different history from that which she has had. But it is interesting to mark how rapidly Calvin's opinions had

---

[117] Ephesians 2:8-10.
[118] Fisher, *History of the Reformation.*
[119] P. 100.

spread in his native land, and to note the evangelistic effect of that system of doctrine which bears his name. Its marvelous evangelizing power lays no doubt in its scriptural thought and phraseology, and its intense spirituality and lofty enthusiasm and logical strength. Luther, though Calvinistic in his doctrinal beliefs, weakened his system by his concessions to princes and ceremonies. He "hesitated," says the historian Bancroft,[120] "to deny the real presence, and was indifferent to the observance of external ceremonies. Calvin, with sterner dialectics, sanctioned by the influence of the purest life and by his power as the ablest writer of his age, attacked the Roman doctrine respecting communion, and esteemed as a commemoration a rite which the Catholics revered as a sacrifice. Luther acknowledged princes as his protectors, and in the ceremonies of worship favored magnificence as an aid to devotion; Calvin was the guide of Swiss republics, and avoided, in their churches, all appeals to the senses as a crime against religion . . . Luther permitted the cross and taper, pictures and images, as things of indifference. Calvin demanded a spiritual worship in its utmost purity." Hence it was that Calvinism, by bringing the truth directly to bear upon the mind and heart, made its greater and more permanent conquests, and subjected itself to the fiercer opposition and persecution of Romanism.

"The Lutheran Reformation," says Dyer[121] in his *History of Modern Europe*, "traveled but little out of Germany and the neighboring Scandinavian kingdoms; while Calvinism obtained a European character, and was adopted in all the countries that adopted a reformation from without, as France, as the Netherlands, Scotland, even England; for the early English Reformation under Edward VI was Calvinistic, and Calvin was incontestably

---

[120] *History of the United States*, vol. I, pp, 277, 278.
[121] Thomas Henry Dyer, *History of Modern Europe*, vol. ii, p. 7.

the father of our Puritans and dissenters. Thus, under his rule, Geneva may be said to have become the capital of European Reform."

A similar testimony is that of Francis de Sales, who in one of his letters to the duke of Savoy urged the suppression of Geneva as the capital of what the Romish Church calls heresy. "All the heretics," said he, "respect Geneva as the asylum of their religion . . . There is not a city in Europe which offers more facilities for the encouragement of heresy, for it is the gate of France, of Italy and Germany, so that one finds there people of all nations— Italians, French, Germans, Poles, Spaniards, English, and of countries still more remote. Besides, every one knows the great number of ministers bred there. Last year it furnished twenty to France. Even England obtains ministers from Geneva. What shall I say of its magnificent printing establishments, by means of which the city floods the world with its wicked books, and even goes the length of distributing them at the public expense? . . All the enterprises undertaken against the Holy See and the Catholic princes have their beginnings at Geneva. No city in Europe receives more apostates of all grades, secular and regular. From thence I conclude that Geneva being destroyed would naturally lead to the dissipation of heresy."[122]

God had ordered it that Geneva, so accessible to all the nations of Western Europe, should be the home of Calvin, from which he could most efficiently carry on his work of enlightenment and civilization. And so important to the cause of Protestantism had that city become that upon it, in the opinion of Francis de Sales, the whole cause depended.

Almost marvelous indeed was the rapid spread of the doctrines of Calvinism. Dyer says: "Calvinism, still more

---

[122] *Vie de Ste. Francois de Sales, par son neveu*, p. 120.

inimical to Rome than the doctrines of Luther had, from Geneva, its centre and stronghold, spread itself in all directions in Western Europe. In the neighboring provinces of Germany it had in a great degree supplanted Lutheranism, and had even penetrated into Hungary and Poland; it was predominant in Scotland, and had leavened the doctrines of the English Church . . . The pope could reckon only upon Spain and Italy as sound and secure, with a few islands and the Venetian provinces in Dalmatia and Greece . . . Its converts belonged chiefly (in France) to the higher ranks, including many of the clergy, monks, nuns, and even bishops; and the Catholic churches seemed almost deserted, except by the lower classes."[123]

From this brief survey we are enabled to perceive something of the wonderful evangelizing force of this system of belief. It was the only system able to cope with the great powers of the Romish Church, and overthrow them; and for two centuries it was accepted in all Protestant countries as the final account of the relations between man and his Maker."[124] In fact, there is no other system which has displayed so powerful an evangelizing force as Calvinism.

This becomes still more manifest in the history of the great revivals with which the Christian Church has been blessed.

Many are accustomed to think that revivals belong particularly to the Methodist Church, whereas, in fact, that Church has never yet inaugurated a great national or far-spreading revival. Her revivals are marked with localism; they are connected with particular churches, and do not make a deep, abiding and general impression on society. The first great Christian revival occurred under the preaching of Peter in Jerusalem, who employed such

---

[123] *History of Modern Europe*, vol. ii, pp. 136, 392.
[124] Froude, *Calvinism*, p. 4.

language in his discourse or discourses as this: "Him, being delivered by the determinate counsel and foreknowledge of God, ye have taken, and by wicked hands have crucified and slain."[125] That is Calvinism rigid enough. Passing over the greatest revival of modern times, the Reformation, which, as all know, was under the preaching of Calvinism, we come to our own land. The era of revivals in this country is usually reckoned from the year 1792, but in 1740 there was a marked revival under the preaching of the Rev. Jonathan Dickinson, a Presbyterian clergyman. It was about this time also that George Whitefield, called in his day "the great Methodist," a clergyman of the Church of England and an uncompromising Calvinist, was startling the ungodly in Philadelphia. It is recorded that he threw "a horrid gloom" over this fashionable and worldly old town, "and put a stop to the dancing-schools, assemblies and every pleasant thing." Strange, indeed, that dissipation and vanity are "pleasant things," while holiness and salvation from hell are disagreeable things! But this great man, in company with Gilbert Tennent, a Presbyterian clergyman, of whom Whitefield said, "He is a son of thunder," and "hypocrites must either soon be converted or enraged at his preaching," was arousing multitudes by his fiery, impassioned, consecrated eloquence. We speak of the Methodist Church beginning in a revival. And so it did. But the first and chief actor in that revival was not Wesley, but Whitefield. Though a younger man than Wesley, it was he who first went forth preaching in the fields and gathering multitudes of followers, and raising money and building chapels. It was Whitefield who invoked the two Wesleys to his aid. And he had to employ much argument and persuasion to overcome their prejudices against the movement. Whitefield began the

---

[125] Acts 2:23

111

great work at Bristol and Kingswood, and had found thousands flocking to his side, ready to be organized into churches, when he appealed to Wesley for assistance. Wesley, with all his zeal, had been quite a High-Churchman in many of his views. He believed in immersing even the infants, and demanded that dissenters should be re-baptized before being taken into the Church. He could not think of preaching in any place but in a church. "He should have thought," as he said, "the saving of souls almost a sin if it had not been done in a church."[126] Hence when Whitefield called on John Wesley to engage with him in the popular movement, he shrank back. Finally, he yielded to Whitefield's persuasions, but, he allowed himself to be governed in the decision by what many would regard as a superstition. He and Charles first opened their Bibles at random to see if their eyes should fall on a text which might decide them. But the texts were all foreign to the subject. Then he had recourse to sortilege and cast lots to decide the matter. The lot drawn was the one marked for him to consent, and so he consented. Thus he was led to undertake the work with which his name has been so intimately and honorably associated ever since.

So largely was the Methodist movement owing to Whitefleld that he was called "the Calvinistic establisher of Methodism," and to the end of his life he remained the representative of it in the eyes of the learned world. Horace Walpole, in his *Letters,* speaks only once of Wesley in connection with the rise of Methodism, while he frequently speaks of Whitefield in connection with it. Richard Mant, in his course of lectures against Methodism, speaks of it as an entirely Calvinistic affair.[127] Neither the mechanism nor the force which gave rise to it

---

[126] Lecky, *History of England, Eighteenth Century*, vol. ii. p. 612.
[127] *Bampton Lectures*, for 1812.

originated with Wesley.[128] Field-preaching, which gave
the whole movement its aggressive character, and fitted
and enabled it to cope with the powerful agencies which
were armed against it, was begun by Whitefleld, whilst
"Wesley was dragged into it reluctantly." In the polite
language of the day "Calvinism" and "Methodism" were
synonymous terms, and the Methodists were called
"another sect of Presbyterians."[129] The sainted Toplady
said of the time, "Arminianism is the great religious evil
of this age and country. It has more or less infected every
Protestant denomination amongst us, and bids fair for
leaving us, in a short time, not so much as the very
profession of godliness . . . We have generally forsaken
the principles of the Reformation, and 'Ichabod,' *the glory
is departed,* has been written on most of our pulpits and
church-doors ever since."

It was Calvinism, and not Arminianism, which originated (so far as any system of doctrines originated) the
great religious movement in which the Methodist Church
was born.

While, therefore, Wesley is to be honored for his work
in behalf of that Church, we should not fail to remember
the great Calvinist, George Whitefield, who gave that
Church her first beginnings and her most distinctive
character. Had he lived longer, and not shrunk from the
thought of being the founder of a Church, far different
would have been the results of his labors. As it was, he
gathered congregations for others to form into churches,
and built chapels for others to preach in.

In all that awakening in this country it were such
Calvinists as Whitefleld, Tennent, Edwards, Brainerd, and,
at a later day, Nettleton and Griffin, who were the chief
actors. "The Great Revival of 1800," as it is called, began

---

[128] Josiah Wedgewood's *Life of John Wesley*, p. 157.
[129] *Bampton Lectures*, for 1812.

toward the close of the last century and continued for a generation into this. During that time it was one series of awakenings. It spread far and wide, refreshing and multiplying the churches. It was the be-ginning of all those great religious movements for which our century is so noted. The doctrines which were employed to bring it about were those, as a recent writer remarks, "Which are commonly distinguished as Calvinistic."[130] "The work," says another, "was begun and carried on in this country under the preaching and influence of the doctrines contained in the Confession of Faith of the Presbyterian Church."[131] "It is wonderful how the holy influence of Jonathan Edwards, David Brainerd and others of that day is to be traced at the root of the revival and missionary efforts of *all sects and lands.*"[132]

The revival which began in New England, and which was the greatest that had, until that time, been witnessed in the American colonies, resulted, under the blessing of God, from a series of doctrinal sermons preached by Jonathan Edwards.

But I cannot continue to specify instances. Let it be borne in mind that the men who have awakened the consciences and swayed the masses, and brought the multitudes to the feet of Jesus, not in a temporary ex-citement, but in a perpetual covenant, have been such Calvinists as Ambrose Willie, and John Knox, and Thomas Chalmers, and George Whitefield, and Jonathan Edwards, and Griffin, Nettleton, Moody, and, last but not least, Spurgeon.

Calvinism may be unpopular in some quarters. But what of that? It cannot be more unpopular than the doctrines of sin and grace as revealed in the New Tes-

---

[130] Dr. William Speer's, *Great Revival of 1800*, p. 52.
[131] Dr. Smil. Ralston's *Letters*.
[132] Speer's *Great Revival*, p. 112.

tament. But much of its unpopularity is due to the fact of its not being understood. Let it be examined without passion, let it be studied in its relations and logical consistency, and it will be seen to be at least a correct transcript of the teachings of the Scriptures, of the laws of Nature and of the facts of human life. If the faith and piety of the Church be weak today, it is, I am convinced, in a great measure because of the lack of a full, clear, definite knowledge and promulgation of these doctrines. The Church has been having a reign of *candyism;* she has been feeding on pap sweetened with treacle, until she has become disordered and weakly. Give her a more clearly-defined and a more firmly-grasped faith, and she will lift herself up in her glorious might before the world.

All history and experience prove the correctness of Carlyle's saying, that "At all turns a man who will *do* faithfully needs to *believe firmly.*" It is this, I believe, that the Church needs today more than any other thing—not "rain-doctors," not religious "diviners," wandering to and fro, rejoicing in having no dogmatic opinions and no theological preferences; no, it is not these religious ear-ticklers that are *needed*—although they may be wanted somewhere—but, as history teaches us, clear and accurate views of the great fundamental doctrines of sin and grace. First make the tree good, and the fruit will be good. A good tree cannot bring forth evil fruit. It is not for us to trifle with these matters. Our time here is but for a moment, and our eternity depends on the course we take. Should we not, then, seek to know the truth, and strive, at any cost, to buy it, and sell it not?

By all the terrors of an endless death, as by all the glories of an endless life, we are called and pressed and urged to know the truth and follow it unto the end. And this joy we have, in and over all as the presence of a divine radiance, "that He which hath begun a good work in you will perform it until the day of Jesus Christ." So grant thou Holy Spirit of God, to begin the work in every one of us; and to Thee, with the Father and the Son, shall be all the praise and the glory for ever! Amen.

Other SGCB Classic Reprints

In addition to *Calvinism in History* which you now hold in your hands, Solid Ground Christian Books is honored to present the following titles, many for the first time in more than a century:

THEOLOGY ON FIRE: *Sermons from the Heart of J.A. Alexander*

A SHEPHERD'S HEART: *Sermons from the Ministry of J.W. Alexander*

EVANGELICAL TRUTH: *Sermons for the Christian Home by A. Alexander*

OPENING SCRIPTURE: *A Hermeneutical Manual by Patrick Fairbairn*

THE ASSURANCE OF FAITH *by Louis Berkhof*

THE PASTOR IN THE SICK ROOM *by John D. Wells*

THE BUNYAN OF BROOKLYN: *The Life & Sermons of Ichabod Spencer*

THE NATIONAL PREACHER: *Sermons from the 2nd Great Awakening*

THE POOR MAN'S OT COMMENTARY *by Robert Hawker* (6 vols)

THE POOR MAN'S NT COMMENTARY *by Robert Hawker* (3 vols)

FIRST THINGS: *The First Lessons God Taught Mankind by Gardiner Spring*

BIBLICAL & THEOLOGICAL STUDIES *by the 1912 Faculty of Princeton*

THE POWER OF GOD UNTO SALVATION *by B.B. Warfield*

THE LORD OF GLORY *by B.B. Warfield*

A GENTLEMAN & A SCHOLAR: *Memoir of J.P. Boyce by John Broadus*

SERMONS TO THE NATURAL MAN *by W.G.T. Shedd*

SERMONS TO THE SPIRITUAL MAN *by W.G.T. Shedd*

HOMILETICS AND PASTORAL THEOLOGY *by W.G.T. Shedd*

A PASTOR'S SKETCHES 1 & 2 *by Ichabod S. Spencer*

THE PREACHER AND HIS MODELS *by James Stalker*

IMAGO CHRISTI *by James Stalker*

A HISTORY OF PREACHING *by Edwin C. Dargan*

LECTURES ON THE HISTORY OF PREACHING *by John A. Broadus*

THE SCOTTISH PULPIT *by William Taylor*

THE SHORTER CATECHISM ILLUSTRATED *by John Whitecross*

THE CHURCH MEMBER'S GUIDE *by John Angell James*

THE SUNDAY SCHOOL TEACHER'S GUIDE *by John Angell James*

CHRIST IN SONG: *Hymns of Immanuel from All Ages by Philip Schaff*

COME YE APART: *Daily Words from the Four Gospels by J.R. Miller*

DEVOTIONAL LIFE OF THE S.S. TEACHER *by J.R. Miller*

Call us Toll Free at 1-877-666-9469
Send us an e-mail at sgcb@charter.net
Visit us on line at solid-ground-books.com

Uncovering Buried Treasure to the Glory of God